On-Camera Coach

Tools and Techniques for Business Professionals in a Video-Driven World

Wiley & SAS Business Series

The Wiley & SAS Business Series presents books that help senior-level managers with their critical management decisions.

Titles in the Wiley & SAS Business Series include:

Developing Human Capital: Using Analytics to Plan and Optimize Your Learning and Development Investments by Gene Pease, Barbara Beresford, and Lew Walker

The Executive's Guide to Enterprise Social Media Strategy: How Social Networks Are Radically Transforming Your Business by David Thomas and Mike Barlow

Economic and Business Forecasting: Analyzing and Interpreting Econometric Results by John Silvia, Azhar Iqbal, Kaylyn Swankoski, Sarah Watt, and Sam Bullard

Economic Modeling in the Post Great Recession Era: Incomplete Data, Imperfect Markets by John Silvia, Azhar Iqbal, and Sarah Watt House

Foreign Currency Financial Reporting from Euros to Yen to Yuan: A Guide to Fundamental Concepts and Practical Applications by Robert Rowan

Harness Oil and Gas Big Data with Analytics: Optimize Exploration and Production with Data Driven Models by Keith Holdaway

Health Analytics: Gaining the Insights to Transform Health Care by Jason Burke

Heuristics in Analytics: A Practical Perspective of What Influences Our Analytical World by Carlos Andre Reis Pinheiro and Fiona McNeill

Human Capital Analytics: How to Harness the Potential of Your Organization's Greatest Asset by Gene Pease, Boyce Byerly, and Jac Fitz-enz

Implement, Improve and Expand Your Statewide Longitudinal Data System: Creating a Culture of Data in Education by Jamie McQuiggan and Armistead Sapp

Intelligent Credit Scoring: Building and Implementing Better Credit Risk Scorecards, Second Edition by Naeem Siddiqi

Killer Analytics: Top 20 Metrics Missing from your Balance Sheet by Mark Brown

On-Camera Coach: Tools and Techniques for Business Professionals in a Video-Driven World by Karin Reed

Predictive Analytics for Human Resources by Jac Fitz-enz and John Mattox II

For more information on any of the above titles, please visit www.wiley.com.

On-Camera Coach

Tools and Techniques for Business
Professionals in a Video-Driven World

Karin Reed

WILEY

For general information on our other products and services or for technical
support, please contact our Customer Care Department within the United
States at (800) 762-2974, outside the United States at (317) 572-3993 or fax
(317) 572-4002.

Wiley publishes in a variety of print and electronic formats and by print-on-
demand. Some material included with standard print versions of this book
may not be included in e-books or in print-on-demand. If this book refers to
media such as a CD or DVD that is not included in the version you purchased,
you may download this material at http://booksupport.wiley.com. For more
information about Wiley products, visit www.wiley.com.

Library of Congress Cataloging-in-Publication Data:

ISBN 9781119316039 (Hardcover)
ISBN 9781119324720 (ePDF)
ISBN 9781119324713 (ePub)

Printed in the United States of America

10 9 8 7 6 5 4 3 2 1

For Dad—my favorite writer of all

Contents

Preface

For the business executive of today—and surely of tomorrow—being able to communicate through a camera is an essential skill. It's powerful. It's immediate. It's often necessary to reach global audiences.

It's never been easier to leverage video across the corporate landscape to reach both internal and external audiences. Cameras are no longer confined to studios or designated videoconference rooms; they're on our phones, our laptops, and our tablets. A face-to-face meeting with a client on the other side of the world may require only a video chat app and a strong Wi-Fi network.

But speaking to a camera is not like speaking to a roomful of people you can actually see. It requires an entirely different skill set—one most people don't innately possess. This book aims to take the mystery out of communicating through the camera and provide specific tips and techniques that can make your message sing—and you, the messenger, feel confident in a job well done.

If you have comments or questions—or simply want more information on live training, feel free to contact us at Info@SpeakerDyamics.com.

Acknowledgments

A heartfelt thank you to all of my clients who have had the courage to step in front of the camera and learn how to speak through it, not shrink from it. I have learned as much from you as I hope you have learned from me.

If Kathy Council, Vice President of Publications at SAS, had not taken my on-camera performance class, I am quite certain this book would never have existed. Thank you, Kathy, for encouraging me to pursue putting it in print. Additional gratitude goes to Shelly Sessoms and Stacey Hamilton for ushering it through on the SAS side.

Thanks to Vicki Bevenour, Ian Ziskin, and Bill Franks, fellow authors who assured me I could climb this mountain and suggested ways to navigate it with ease.

For their time and expertise, I want to thank Jeffery West, Brad Simmons, and Andrew Davis. Your expert insight was much appreciated.

It was an honor to have my former vocal coach, Dr. Candice Coleman, help shape my content related to Analytical Reading. Candy, your contributions were invaluable.

Kathi Duggan, editor extraordinaire, thank you for guiding me through the editing process with a deft hand and a winning sense of humor. Can I send *all* of my professional copy to you? This is a lifelong relationship, right? Additional thanks to Sheck Cho and Judy Howarth at Wiley for your support and answers to even my inane questions.

To my family, thank you for allowing me to be consumed by the creation of this book. Shawn, Hayden, and Jackson—you know I love you beyond words.

Finally, to my mom, Peggy, my first and biggest fan—thank you for always thinking my writing has been worthy of a Pulitzer. (Honestly, my seventh grade autobiography wasn't that great, Mom.) Much love.

On-Camera Coach

*Tools and Techniques for Business
Professionals in a Video-Driven World*

The Inescapable Reality—We *All* Have to Communicate through a Camera

It used to be unusual to be caught on tape, but today, cameras are everywhere, even in the palms of our hands. We use them to communicate with our family and friends, and more and more often, with our coworkers or customers. The reason for this is that video is immediate, impactful, and increasingly more accessible.

In this section, you will learn how communicating through a camera is becoming an essential business skill and why the barriers to doing it well are considerable. The section is divided into the following two chapters:

- Chapter 1: Why You Need to Read This Book
- Chapter 2: Why the Camera Changes Everything

CHAPTER **1**

Why You Need to Read This Book

Gladys and her girls

D on't let the sunshine yellow suit fool you. This is the unapologeti-
cally unhappy face of a woman who does not like cameras.

The unfortunate circumstance for my nana, Gladys Mason:
her beloved husband was what we'd now call "an early adopter." The
movements of my mother's side of the family were well documented
on film, and the Martin Scorsese behind the movie camera was my
grandfather, Harry.

Gladys was a frequent if unwilling participant in his 8mm films,
so consequently, we all became intimately familiar with certain angles
and parts of her body—the back of her head, perhaps a quick glimpse
of the side of her face as she pivoted away from the offending lens
before running rabbit to a faraway glen. If she couldn't dash away,
she would try to hide in plain sight by extending her palm toward the

camera, precursor to the paparazzi pose seen on the covers of tabloids the world over.

The good news for Gladys? For the most part, she only had to juke out my movie-making Papa to maintain her credentials as a Professional Camera Avoider. For the most part, Papa brought his camera out only for special occasions: family reunions, the first day of school, holidays. (On Christmas morning, no one was allowed to come downstairs to see what Santa brought until the room was properly illuminated by his own massive bank of lights. True.)

But today, avoiding Papa's lens would be the least of Gladys's concerns. Cameras are everywhere. I shudder when I imagine the levels of panic she would hit today.

THE POWER AND PERVASIVENESS OF VIDEO

Video cameras are no longer just in a studio or pulled out of the closet for dance recitals; they're on your laptop, your webcam, your phone. They invade your personal space through apps like Skype, FaceTime, and Google Hangouts, and they've become as ubiquitous in the workplace as Excel spreadsheets and leftover birthday cake.

So what's driving this video proliferation? The medium itself is powerful and personal.

Consider how much time you spend viewing videos today versus even five years ago. The Age of YouTube has created an expectation that you can always watch rather than read. Need to know how to install a garbage disposal? Well, you *could* follow the directions enclosed in the Home Depot box—but why do that, when you can watch Bob the Plumber show you step by step in his DIY video?

Millennials have upped the ante even more with a penchant for Snapchat selfies and conversations conducted at length through the ever-growing list of video chat apps. For that generation, communicating through a camera is almost second nature.

But even the stodgiest of corporate cultures are making room for video. Corporate YouTube and Vimeo channels, Twitter accounts, and myriad social media opportunities vie with webinars, videoconferences, and Ted Talks for content. If a corporate web site doesn't have a video component, it looks outdated and downright boring. For the marketing department, it's a virtual video smorgasbord with unprecedented avenues to get your message out there.

But what happens if your messenger is about as dynamic on camera as a ham sandwich?

THE DECLINE OF THE PROFESSIONAL SPOKESPERSON

After a successful 15-year career in television news, I left the business after one too many "team coverage" snow-mageddon events, holidays spent on set and middle-of-the-night phone calls to cover whatever news was breaking. I moved to what I called "The Dark Side"—doing on-camera and voice-over work for any corporation interested in hiring me to serve as its professional spokesperson. I quickly realized how transferable and in demand my skills would be. Video is pervasive throughout the corporate landscape.

However, over the past decade of doing this kind of work, I have noticed a trend. More and more companies are forgoing the "professional spokesperson/actor" and are instead opting to put their "real" employees on camera, people who usually have had no prior experience or training in how to communicate through a camera. To me, that's unequivocally unfair.

I have spent more than 20 years honing my skills in front of the camera and have discovered what works and what doesn't, often through trial and error. My first stint in TV news was at a CBS affiliate in Youngstown, Ohio. Who knows why the news director hired me to be the weekend reporter and weather anchor? Perhaps it had something to do with the fact that I said I would do this for free. (They did pay me, and as a senior in college, I considered it more than adequate. Heck, I lived on Taco Bell.) I was awful on camera initially, but I learned my craft and eventually became a well-respected, award-winning journalist and anchor.

The only training most of these corporate execs have had is a quick reminder to smile right before the red light goes on. And yet hiring someone like me to be the mouthpiece for the enterprise is becoming less and less common.

Blame it on Steve Jobs for helping to create this age of the celebrity CEO, but be aware that the days of sending out the professional spokesperson are numbered. Your customers, your employees, and just about anyone else who is watching your video will want to hear from the decision makers, the doers, the C-suite executives—and more and more often, that means speaking on camera.

THE GLOBAL COMMUNICATION TOOL OF CHOICE

Video is a vital communication link for a workforce that is often not corralled within the bricks and mortar of the corporate monolith. It's immediate and impactful, and it can save you a ton of money.

Important enterprise-wide announcements are regularly taped and uploaded to an organization's intranet. Training that once was held at the home office is now delivered through video portals. Colleagues can now collaborate across continents with greater ease, albeit with less sleep for those whose time zone received short shrift.

Videoconferencing is not new. It's been around for decades, but for the majority of those years, the technology was siloed in specific rooms, which were hard to book, and usually reserved for the C-suite and senior-level executives. Today, videoconferencing has come to the masses, whenever and wherever they are.

While the teleconference still holds a firm majority, videoconferencing is growing in popularity at a rapid rate. According to a Wainhouse Research survey in 2015, respondents indicated an average of 42 percent of their Web conferences involved video.[1]

Additional insight from Wainhouse Research indicates that those who are already active users of videoconferencing are deepening their commitment to it. Of the roughly 170 respondents, 97 percent said they use videoconferencing more now than they did two years ago, and nearly the same high percentage of respondents pointed to improvements in reliability (95 percent) and ease of use (92 percent). According to that Wainhouse report, "Companies around the world are depending on video-enabled meetings to empower their people, serve clients better, and compete on a global basis."[2]

The advantages of videoconferencing are both tangible and intangible. For employees who are far-flung, virtual video meetings provide an acceptable and often preferred alternative to traveling to a meeting on site. It saves on costs and downtime due to travel, increasing productivity.

Introducing a visual element also has the effect of turning a virtual meeting into one where etiquette mimics that of an in-room meeting. Remember the YouTube video that went viral, showing what really happens during conference calls? (If you haven't, search "Conference Call in Real Life" on YouTube.) Turning webcams on minimizes multitasking. Checking e-mail, playing solitaire, or grabbing a latte at your favorite coffeehouse becomes much more difficult to pull off if your face is constantly visible to all parties. The result? Everyone is forced to focus but rewarded by a meeting that is often shorter.

Video meetings can be more meaningful, too. It's easier to build rapport with colleagues and "read the room" when you can see your audience. Body language speaks volumes but is silent on a teleconference call. Videoconferencing allows participants to pick up on nonverbal cues that would have been missed. In addition, research has shown that the majority of us are visual learners, so teleconferencing as a communication tool puts everyone at a disadvantage by forcing us to be primarily auditory learners.

HIRING BY SKYPE

Video chat applications have completely revamped the hiring process across all verticals.

Corporations can cast a much wider net for applicants now that interviewing over the Web is possible. Apps such as Skype, ooVOO, Tango, and Google Hangouts offer an opportunity to connect with potential candidates who may have been eliminated purely based on geography. If someone hits it out of the park during an interview on Google Hangouts, for example, the decision to bring that person in for a face-to-face meeting becomes a much easier one to make. And if there are still reservations, hiring managers can go back and "review the tape," so to speak. Many video chat apps are capable of recording calls or have plug-ins created by other vendors that give users the opportunity to preserve those calls in a digital file.

Video interviews also have the benefit of immediacy. Scheduling a trip to the corporate headquarters can be much more challenging than simply blocking out a chunk of time to chat online. By shortening the time to interview, a company can minimize the time to hire, allowing them to fill key positions quicker and potentially with better-quality candidates thanks to the deeper pool of applicants no longer limited by geography.

THE PERILS OF VIDEO

Want to avoid the camera today? That would be nearly impossible—and a potential professional liability. If *you* don't want to leverage the power of presenting to a camera, someone else will and could be seen as a more valuable asset. Self-promotion can be a strategy, and video provides the perfect platform on which to do it.

But there are risks. Often, the messages being delivered on camera are high stakes: vital news for the entire global enterprise or, even more daunting, for an external audience of customers, competitors, and the always-intimidating media. Performing poorly can undercut the credibility of the presenter and ultimately can hurt the corporate (or personal) brand he or she represents.

By contrast, on-camera expertise can be a true differentiator, especially as the use of video continues its exponential growth. Some camera-savvy corporate folks embrace the opportunity to connect with their audiences in a much deeper way than the written word allows. They come across as authentic and sincere, but that's not the norm.

Most people who do not perform on camera for a living would prefer a root canal. Presenting via video combines two things most people hate: public speaking and being on camera. Even those who are very comfortable speaking to a live audience of hundreds can be flummoxed by having to speak to a single, solitary lens.

HOW READING THIS BOOK CAN IMPROVE YOUR ON-CAMERA PERFORMANCE

The goal of any training is to change either you or the way you do something, but to me, the time spent in the classroom is just the first step. It's purely information transfer. The real "learning" is in the doing. This book is structured to give you not only foundational knowledge, but also ample opportunity to try out the techniques you have learned through specific exercises. Sure, you can skip over them, but your training will only be superficial. You need to practice what you've learned on camera and then evaluate your performance.

It's actually not too difficult to separate the good from the bad when assessing your own performance. Peruse YouTube, and chances are you can easily identify those who have some serious skills in presenting to a camera from those who should have opted for another way (or person) to convey their message. Sometimes, the problems are readily apparent: lightning-fast delivery, distracting gestures, content that is hard to follow. But sometimes, there just seems to be something off. The same can be said of those who are solid performers. You might be thinking, "The camera really loves her," but do you know why? This book will highlight some of the nuances that contribute to performance success and raise your awareness of performance pitfalls that go beyond the obvious.

What You Will Need

In order to assess your performance, you need a way to record yourself, but as you know, cameras surround us. You can use your smartphone, a webcam, or a regular video camera as long as you have a way to review the videos you take with it.

Topics to Be Discussed

The book begins with a discussion of what makes presenting on-camera uniquely challenging and why you are your own worst enemy. We will then take a deep dive into what I call the MVPs of Performance Success. In this book, *MVP* stands for the Mental, Vocal, and Physical elements of performance success. You will hear some case studies from former clients and be given exercises to put those newfound skills into action.

Wondering what to wear on camera? This book will help you comb through your closet for camera-friendly attire that will make you look the part. (An early tip: When in doubt, be boring.)

We will talk about content—both unscripted and scripted—and about the importance of organizing for the ear and writing the way you speak. A great script is the secret sauce for excellent on-camera presentations.

Much of what you will learn can be applied to any formal or informal on-camera performance, whether it's shot in a fancy studio or in your basement. However, I will delve into some tips for specific scenarios like virtual meetings and interviews, formal direct-to-camera presentations, and panel discussions formatted in a broadcast-news style.

Consider this book your on-camera coach: full of tools, techniques, and insight into what works and what doesn't work on camera, no matter where that camera lurks. Many of these tools and techniques can be used in any presentation or performance—whether you can look your audience in the eye or have to imagine them on the other side of a lens.

Feel free to flip to the chapters that best fit your needs, but take note of the topics covered in the other chapters. You never know when you might need to add to your on-camera arsenal.

CHAPTER TAKEAWAYS

- Video cameras are no longer just in a studio; they're on your laptop, your webcam, and your phone.
- The Age of YouTube has created an expectation that you can always watch rather than read.
- Everyone wants to hear from the decision makers, the doers, the C-suite executives . . . and more and more often, that means speaking on camera.
- Video is a vital communication link for a workforce that is often not corralled within the bricks and mortar of the corporate monolith.
- Video chat applications have completely revamped the hiring process across all verticals.
- Performing poorly can undercut the credibility of the presenter and ultimately can hurt the corporate (or personal) brand he or she represents.

NOTES

1. Andrew Davis, *2015 Video Conference End User Survey*, September 2015. http://cp.wainhouse.com/content/2015-video-conferencing-end-user-survey.
2. Ira M. Weinstein and Saar Litman, *Simplicity in the New World of Video Conferencing*, November 2015. http://cp.wainhouse.com/content/simplicity-new-world-video-conferencing.

CHAPTER **2**

Why the Camera Changes Everything

Dateline: Summer 1991

Location: Altoona, Pennsylvania (specifically, Jaffa Shrine)

Event: Final night of competition at the Miss Pennsylvania Scholarship Pageant

I was the season shocker. How could I, Miss Butler County, a pageant neophyte who only entered on a lark, be in prime position to represent the Keystone State in the Miss America pageant?

Talent Competition: I nailed it thanks to a decade of voice training.

Judge's Panel Interview: I aced that, too.

The vast majority of my fellow contestants had been priming themselves for this moment for years, sharpening their skills on the lower-level pageant circuit. Me? I was a total newbie and on no one's radar as a potential threat. But after chalking up two preliminary competition wins earlier in the week, the dark horse had become the front-runner and likely winner . . . save for a slight miscalculation by my team.

You see, along with the tiara from the county win, I had acquired a cadre of pageant professionals who were in charge of coaching me for the state pageant. They taught me how to strut, wobble-free, across the stage in a bathing suit and four-inch heels made of Lucite. They explained the importance of displaying off-the-charts enthusiasm when I introduced myself at the top of the show. We even ran through my song from *Phantom of the Opera* ad nauseam just in case.

What we didn't work on was my on-stage interview question. Why would we? After all, I was a top student and had even skipped my senior year in high school just to get a head start on college. I was on track to receive my undergraduate degree magna cum laude with highest honors. Public speaking was my forte. I even won a scholarship for "Excellence in the Use of the English Language." Why would I need to practice how to answer one question?

So there I was on the final night of the pageant, ready to tackle the last part of the competition: the on-stage interview question. The crowning achievement seemed like a fait accompli.

I made my way downstage toward the emcee, who held a stack of index cards laden with real stumpers—or so he thought. He selected my question.

14

"If money were no object, what would you do to make the world a better place?"

Could there be a bigger softball of a question than that? I'm sure you can think of dozens of answers that would have elicited a round of applause and perhaps even brought a tear to the eye of some touched by your empathy for the needy, the disenfranchised, the unfortunate souls you wanted to help.

My response: "Laughter . . . I'd give the world laughter."

Say what?

There are no "take-backs" when answering a question live before thousands of people in a concert hall and countless others watching on television. I knew I had to find some way to make this substantive despite its laughable start.

I wracked my brain and free-associated laughter with monetary value. After a less than one second pause, I continued my response with this:

"So I'd buy everyone comedians."

My entire entourage from the local pageant collectively slumped in their seats as if they'd been sucker punched.

I knew that I was in the process of completely tanking any chance I had to head to the Miss America Pageant in Atlantic City. Ironically, however, I thought it was hilarious. In fact, I remember trying to stifle a giggle as I fumbled through to the end of my clunker of an answer. There was some polite applause as I walked off stage.

I have to say I was heartened to hear some of the other contestants swing and miss on their questions, too. Here are some of my favorites (with italics added for emphasis by me):

- **Question:** "If you could meet any famous person, living or dead, who would you want to meet?"
  Answer: "Jesus Christ, because he did so much for our *country*."

- **Question:** "If you could live in any *era*, which would you choose?"
  Answer: "I'd live in *the South*, because I really like the warm weather."

So what on earth does this have to do with presenting on camera?

My pageant team assumed that I could handle any interview question thrown my way. Heck, I did, too. *Your* team may assume you can present on camera because you are a solid speaker. And herein lies the problem. Everyone wants to leverage video across all the many channels it now occupies, but very little thought is given to how to use this tool effectively. Too often, business executives are put in front of a camera and expected to perform well without any training. They're obviously intelligent folks who are in their positions of authority based on their achievements. But speaking in front of a camera requires a skill set that is never taught in business school, and very few of us possess the innate ability to do it well.

MY "AHA!" MOMENT

Nowhere was the need for on-camera training more apparent than when I served as a regular webcast moderator for a corporate client. My role was to facilitate the discussion among global thought leaders on the panel. I was largely scripted, which helped me to come across as more knowledgeable than I truly was. What amazed me, though, was the panic many of those brilliant panelists felt just because they were going to be speaking on camera. I thought: *I should be the one who is nervous. You know what the heck you're talking about. I don't.* But I had spent more than two decades both in front of and behind a camera. Without that familiarity, those cameras represented a seismic shift in the environment.

In fact, I thought one of my first gigs as a webcast host was going to be my last. The topic of the show that day was incredibly technical, so my client had brought in an expert with strong credentials and deep domain knowledge. What she lacked, though, was experience communicating through a camera.

I noticed that she looked a little "moist" as we were getting mic'd up, but I had no idea how nervous she really was. In short order, though, it was revealed. I read the introduction of our guest and tossed it over to her for her 30-minute presentation. However, instead of taking the baton and running with it, she simply said, "I can't do this," and attempted to take the mic off her lapel.

Thankfully, this was only the rehearsal. I somehow managed to find the right words to calm her down and convince her to try again. Her performance during the actual show wasn't stellar, but it was much better than no performance at all. (A big shout-out to our makeup artist on that day, who managed to keep the flop sweat mopped up during quick breaks.)

It all boils down to this: there's an assumption that if you can speak to a live audience, you can speak, convincingly and effectively, to a camera lens. And too often, that assumption is proven false, and at the worst possible time.

Unless you have experience performing on camera or are one of those rare people who just takes to it like Tiger Woods to golf, you will want and *need* some strategies, some guidance to perform at your best.

Perhaps if I had tested out some techniques for answering stock pageant questions ("Bring about world peace, feed the hungry . . ." yadda, yadda, yadda), my most embarrassing moment of all time might have been my biggest triumph. (Okay, maybe not *biggest* triumph, but certainly not a complete and utter failure to perform.)

A CAMERA CHANGES EVERYTHING

It may seem odd that the mere presence of a camera can cause such a disruption in the environment and recalibrate the way we act, think, and feel. Often, the change manifests physiologically. As soon as you are told "you're on," your body may send a jolt of adrenaline through you, similar to the one you receive when you stop short in traffic. Your palms may sweat, your knees may knock, and a giant lump may temporarily block your throat.

Why? Allow me to offer four reasons why the camera changes everything.

No Immediate Feedback

When you're giving a presentation to a live audience, you're constantly surveying the room. Maybe you see someone nodding along. Maybe you see someone nodding *off*. You adjust your delivery based on what you see reflected back to you by your audience.

But when you're talking on camera, that lens isn't giving you any indication of whether your message is resonating or even being heard at all. You crave feedback, but the camera doesn't offer anything in return. Basically, it feels like your words are being sucked into a big black hole. That uncertainly can undercut your confidence and cause you to seek out reassurance from any source available.

THE PEOPLE PLEASER

CASE STUDY

Barbara was not a confident on-camera presenter, and yet she knew it was a skill she needed to hone in order to reach her global team.

When Barbara spoke in person, she was known for her warmth, dry sense of humor, and passion for the role her team played in the enterprise. She loved her coworkers, and the feeling was mutual. However, her on-camera persona was a total mismatch with her off-camera self.

Barbara's biggest problem was what I call "People Pleaser Syndrome." Any time she appeared on camera, Barbara's eyes would dart around the studio, desperately seeking out that human interaction and validation for her performance and message. She would try to lock eyes with coworkers who had accompanied her to the shoot and were standing off camera. She would make eye contact with members of the crew. But she rarely looked directly into the camera.

Barbara's urgency to connect with and receive feedback from the people in the room severed any connection she might have had with the real audience: the people watching her performance on the other side of the lens.

Did you ever have a conversation at a cocktail party with someone who is constantly looking around the room for someone "better" to talk to? It makes you feel like you are not valued, right? That's the effect Barbara unwittingly gave her audience by not focusing on them. The "People Pleaser" turned people off.

Your Own Worst Critic

Do you remember when you first heard your voice on your voice mail or answering machine greeting? You probably thought, "I don't sound like that!"

Chances are, what you heard was exactly how your voice sounds—you just didn't like it.

The idea of having to listen to yourself or watch yourself on video can be a painful prospect for many. This is true even for those who do it for a living. When I meet the editors of any of my on-camera jobs, I always offer my sympathy because I know they've had to spend hours upon hours watching and listening to all of my many takes. That's enough to make me nauseous.

I always express my appreciation and admiration for those who take my on-camera performance workshops, because I consider it an act of courage. They are stepping outside of their comfort zones and subjecting themselves to criticism—the sharpest of which comes from within.

Analyzing baseline and post-training performances is an important part of any of my classes, yet it is always met with a cringe. The performers always notice things about themselves that no one else does.

For example, everyone in the class might be applauding your flawless delivery, but you may be totally fixated and irritated by the way your left eyebrow turns slightly downward. While the entire audience is mesmerized by your powerful presentation, you are thinking about how soon you can get in to see the brow lady. A camera lens can sometimes feel like a microscope, but in this case, it usually makes imperfections only we can see loom large.

Recorded for Posterity

Most on-camera performances will or at least can be recorded, and the shelf life of that video, good or bad, will likely be longer than you want it to be. And if your video is going to be hanging out on YouTube for who knows how long, you want it to be *perfect*.

That desire for perfection usually serves as the biggest barrier to performance success. We get incredibly self-conscious, which leads to a tremendous amount of pressure and stress.

For my classes, participants have the option of creating a video asset, which they can use beyond training. It's a valuable opportunity to make the training immediately applicable, but there is a downside.

CASE STUDY

PURSUIT OF PERFECTION

Rob was well ahead of his peers in terms of his comfort and confidence as a presenter, so when he heard he could create a video blog entry as part of the class, he was all for it.

Rob prepared a script in advance of the training and decided to run through it on the first day as his baseline performance. It was a bit bumpy, but he attributed it to problems with his script. Undeterred, he wordsmithed it and practiced it at home before the final record on day two.

When it was his turn to step in front of the camera, Rob felt optimistic and thought he would be able to nail it within one or two takes—a good thing because he was the last of his classmates to perform before their lunch break.

His first run was pretty solid, but he tripped over a couple of words. Take number two started off well, but he stopped in midsentence because he thought he had mispronounced something. (He had not.) Take three turned into four, five, and six in rapid succession, and each failed attempt chipped away at his confidence. Embarrassed by his poor performance, Rob asked if he could come back after lunch to try it again, not wanting to keep his classmates from satiating their appetites.

Although Rob was one of the most skilled of the performers coming into training, his colleagues in the class finished their on-camera presentations in about a third of the time he had spent. The reason for this is that none of Rob's colleagues had exercised the video asset option—whatever they recorded was for training purposes only, so they were willing to cut themselves a little slack. Conversely, Rob was in pursuit of perfection, and the more he pursued it, the more elusive it became.

Unfamiliar Territory

The presence of a camera, even if it's in your own office or home, can immediately transform the familiar into the unfamiliar. Suddenly, you become self-conscious about things you never gave a second thought. What do I do with my hands? Where do I look? What's that hum in the background? This hypersensitivity makes it nearly impossible to perform at your best.

If you are in a studio setting, the otherworldly effect is even more acute. You are surrounded by equipment you have probably never seen and likely find intimidating. There are physical obstructions like cords and wires, which create an obstacle course of a sort, leaving you wondering, "Can I get there from here?" The lights are always brighter than you imagined and cause even the most seasoned performers to initially squint as if it were high noon. Not to mention the whole slew of people who are there, all watching just you.

Why does the camera change everything? Perhaps the question should be "why *wouldn't* the camera change everything?"

THE ARCHENEMY OF PERFORMANCE SUCCESS: YOU

Before we move on, it's important to identify the archenemy of on-camera success. It's not the audience. It's also not the person asking you to go on camera.

It's actually someone who is with you all the time and likely one you are very familiar with: your inner critic. *Every* person has one. Some inner critics are more vocal than others, but that highly critical voice inside your head can derail your performance in big and small ways.

A friend of mine is a drama professor at a university in North Carolina. He told me how he would talk to his class about "the little asshole on your shoulder," that Nagging Nelly who is often responsible for keeping a drama student from fully embodying a role. Call it what you will, that negative force can have a dramatic impact on any performance, whether it's on stage or on camera.

Remember how I talked about the expectation of perfection when you're being recorded? That can cause you to become hyperfocused on any element of your delivery that falls short of that. Say you didn't clearly articulate a sentence or you tripped up on a word. What happens? You start having two conversations: the one that's coming out of your mouth, and the one inside your head between you and your inner critic, who is saying, "Man, that sounded *so* stupid."

When I anchored a newscast, I would wear what's called an IFB, an acronym for interruptible feedback. In layman's terms, it's the earpiece that news anchors wear, which allows the producer or director to talk to him or her throughout the show.

A newscast rarely moves in a linear fashion, especially when there is breaking news. It's the job of the person at the desk to be flexible and adaptable to respond to whatever situation arises without getting flustered. In that circumstance, I would often have three voices inside my head: the one coming out of my mouth, the one belonging to my producer or director via my earpiece, and the one trying to make sense of the directions the producer or director was giving me. ("Drop page six. Go to the reporter live from City Hall. Pitch to the commercial break.")

As a professional, it was my job to always appear serene and in control no matter what chaos was breaking out in the control room. However, keeping my primary focus on the words coming out of my mouth (voice number one) while processing the other voices could be tough. There were times when a producer simply would not stop talking in my ear as I was trying to ad lib through a breaking news situation. If I had all of the information available, I would sometimes simply pull my IFB out of my ear, rendering that producer mute.

Translate that to the conversation you have with your inner critic. Sometimes that inner critic is like the producer who can simply talk too much and distract you from your primary conversation—the one you are having with your viewer.

What do you think happens when your inner critic starts barking at you about some perceived mistake? At worst, you get flustered and *really* start to mess up. At best, you start to go on autopilot. Instead of concentrating on delivering your message with passion and impact, half of your attention is devoted to what happened minutes ago. And your audience will know it. Even a subtle shift in focus can be seen all over your face.

So how do you keep your inner critic from hijacking your performance? Force yourself to stay in the moment and cut yourself some slack. The sooner you forget your perceived mistake, the sooner your audience will, too. It's often a much bigger deal to you than it is to them anyway.

THE KEY TO ON-CAMERA SUCCESS: AUTHENTICITY

Often, the most effective on-camera communicators are those who seem genuine, not those who seem like they're "performing" but those who seem to be just talking to you. The camera exaggerates a lack of authenticity, so the goal is for you to be *yourself*—albeit your *best* self.

Now this can run counter to advice given by other communication coaches and trainers. I found this out firsthand.

On-camera performance training is not nearly as common as traditional presentation training designed for presentations delivered to an audience in the same room. As a result, many of my students come into my class with a toolbox of techniques taught to them by other communication professionals. There may be overlap: some of my strategies align with what they've been taught, which serves to solidify the key learnings. However, there have been plenty of times where I've seen a one-size-fits-all approach backfire and strip all authenticity away from the presenter.

LOSE THE TWANG?

CASE STUDY

Mike was personable and downright hilarious, with a gift for telling stories, which kept you in stitches and hooked on his every word. Thanks to a fairly thick southern accent, his long syllables and drawn out sentences only added to the effect.

When he started my class, he asked how he could "get rid" of his accent. I couldn't figure out why on earth he would be asking that question. His accent was an essential part of his personal style. He explained to me that a presentation coach had told him it was necessary for him to lose his accent in order to be credible.

This communication coach had a system of do's and don'ts, which he strongly encouraged everyone to follow. It included everything from what five gestures are allowed to what pattern of speech to employ. You can imagine how delighted some of those in the class were. They knew they needed to be better presenters, and this list of rules was almost like finding the Golden Egg.

For Mike, some of these "rules" felt awkward when put into practice, including the suggestion that he lose his accent. Plus, Mike had no idea how to even begin the process.

I assured Mike that his accent was not a problem. It wasn't a barrier to audience comprehension. He articulated each word just fine. The true problem would be if he tried to eliminate his accent, which helped define him. He would lose the authenticity that allows him to captivate and connect with his audience, in person and on camera.

I believe the best presenters are steeped in authenticity, not prefab polish. Throughout this book, you will learn techniques, but know that while some of them may and hopefully will work for you, some may not. That's perfectly fine and to be expected. The goal is not to create on-camera automatons that all use the same gestures and same pattern of speech.

The goal is to help you find your own performance style, which maximizes your personal strengths and remains true to who you are, off camera. Try out the techniques discussed, but if they feel false, do *not* use them. Your gut is a powerful truth teller and will help you preserve that authentic self required to truly communicate through the camera.

CHAPTER TAKEAWAYS

A camera changes everything because

- It offers no feedback, so there is no way to judge how the message is being received.
- No one likes how he or she looks or sounds on camera, so there is an automatic aversion to the final product.
- Performers want perfection because it is being recorded and will have a long shelf life.
- It makes even the familiar seem unfamiliar and uncomfortable.
- The archenemy of on-camera success is your inner critic, whose harsh judgments can derail any performance.
- Authenticity is the key to on-camera success. The goal is to be yourself—your *best* self.

The MVPs of Performance Success

So how do you silence the inner critic?

Knowing some basic tricks of the trade may not completely silence the inner critic, but they can at least help you turn down the volume.

I based the MVPs of Performance Success covered in this book on my more than two decades of experience spent in front of a camera. They serve as a way to categorize the wide array of techniques you can employ while communicating through a camera. As mentioned in Chapter 1, the acronym MVP in this technique refers to the Mental, Vocal, and Physical elements of performance, and all of these need to be working in concert to maximize your impact.

This section will go over each element in detail and highlight potential pitfalls along with proven solutions. It is divided into the following three chapters:

- Chapter 3: *M*—Mental Mind-Set: The Prep before the Performance
- Chapter 4: *V*—Vocal Variety: Pacing and Pausing with Purpose
- Chapter 5: *P*—Physical Factors: On-Camera Movement with Meaning

CHAPTER **3**

M—Mental Mind-set: The Prep before the Performance

REACHING THE *REAL* AUDIENCE

When you speak directly to a camera, how many people do you think you are talking to?

You might say, "Well, it depends." After all, your performance could be viewed by a roomful of people or an individual sitting at his or her desk. While this is true in a literal sense, it is not true in a conceptual way, and it brings us to a key difference when presenting to a camera: It is always an audience of one.

No matter how many people may be watching your performance at any given time, every person feels like you are talking to just him or her. The conversation between you and your viewer is very intimate— more like talking to someone across the dinner table than from up on stage. That key mental concept dictates everything you do.

Imagine if someone spoke to you across the dinner table as if he was speaking from behind a podium. He might appear full of bombast, out of touch with what is appropriate for the setting. Many people who have tried to translate their formal presentation skills to on-camera performance fail for this very reason.

You have to understand the closeness of the on-camera conversation and respect its boundaries. If you talk *at* your audience, you risk turning them off and having them tune you out. Instead, you should talk *with* them, as if you were having a conversation with a friend or colleague.

THE NEWS ANCHOR NEXT DOOR

CASE STUDY

As a news anchor, I was welcomed into thousands of homes on a daily basis, which created a deeper bond with my viewers than I could have imagined. This bond manifested in various ways. Some were delightful: boxes full of baby gifts sent to the station when I was obviously expecting, even hand-knitted hats and socks. Others, not so much.

If I went to the grocery store or out to a restaurant, people would often come up to me and greet me like an old friend. After all, I did come into their living rooms on a nearly daily basis and chat for a good hour of their day. The fact that it was a one-sided conversation didn't really matter much to them. They thought they knew me, intimately, so that gave them license to tell me just how they felt about all sorts of things—especially my appearance. Here are a couple of the more *endearing* comments I received:

> **Viewer:** "You look so different in person."
>> **How I wanted to respond:** "Different good or different bad?"
>> **What I actually said:** "Oh, really. That's interesting."
> **Viewer:** "Why does your nose look so big on TV?"
>> **How I wanted to respond:** "I don't know. Why are you ugly in person?"
>> **What I actually said:** "Oh, you know what they say—the camera always adds 10 pounds."

No matter how rude the question, I always responded politely and listened to them tell me about their families, their jobs, or whatever was on their minds. That's what good friends do, right?

Occasionally, that intimate relationship would pay off in a professional sense.

Case in point: I was given the assignment of a noon live shot where I would report from the scene of a brutal attempted murder that happened the night before. When my photographer and I arrived at the location, I decided to walk up the stairs of the triple-decker to the third floor and knock on the door of the apartment where the crime occurred.

To those who aren't in the business, this may sound nuts. You have a point. However, I was young reporter determined to take the extra step— or in this case, many steps—to get the story.

I did have a moment of hesitation due to the bullet holes in the wooden door, but then I went ahead and knocked anyway. Would anyone be home? Would I be told to get out, in no uncertain terms?

None of those things happened; instead, I was greeted by a 20-year-old guy in a wife-beater T-shirt, who exclaimed, "Karin Reed!!! Come on in!!!"

He proceeded to enthusiastically give me a tour of the apartment, which included a show-and-tell of the very room where the assault happened— bloodstains and all.

This may not sound like a professional coup, but in my world, it was, and it was made possible by the fact that I had already been in that apartment many, many times—via their television. They felt like they knew me, so they felt comfortable inviting me in. (Lucky me, huh?)

Visualize the Viewer

Now that you understand the psychology behind the relationship you have with your viewer, let's talk about how you can put the knowledge into action to improve your performance. We have already established that your audience is not the camera, but rather the person who is watching you on the other side of that lens—the person you can't see. ... Or can you?

One of the best ways to bridge the gap is to try to visualize one viewer. Before any on-camera performance, think about someone who might be watching you and consider what tone you would likely strike with him or her. Your visualized viewer might be a member of your team if you're delivering an internal message. Perhaps the message is going out to a pool of potential clients? Visualize one of those customers. When you get in front of the camera, speak to that person just as you would as if he or she were in the same room with you.

If you are in a formal studio setting, you may have a few more options. If someone is standing behind the camera, you can talk to the camera operator. Your view of him or her might be impeded, but it could be an easier mental leap for you if the visualized viewer is in the same room. Just don't expect the camera operator to talk back.

Sometimes when I anchor webcasts for a particular corporate client, I focus on speaking to the director of the show even though I can't see him. Before the webcast, the director and I usually banter about sports, a mutual passion, and I always look directly into the camera during these chats. My reason for doing this is that I know he is in the control room looking at my face in the monitor, and I am creating virtual eye contact. Weird but true. These pre-performance conversations help me to get into the proper mental mind-set.

Video Chat: Now You See Me, Now You Don't

A video chat might seem like an easier scenario to handle because you don't have to visualize a pseudo viewer, but actually it can be even more challenging.

Yes, you can see your audience, and yes, they can see you. However, there is a huge obstacle to effective communication—imprecise eye contact. Unless you are using a system where the camera is implanted in the screen, you will not be able to look your conversation partner in the eye, especially if it is involving only two people.

Typical video chat apps show the person you are talking to in a much bigger window than the one in which you appear. Our natural inclination is to make eye contact with that person. Unfortunately, when we do that, our eye line is significantly lower and we appear to be looking down. In fact, it can make us look like we are avoiding eye contact altogether.

Don't believe me? Check it out for yourself. Conduct a video chat with a family member or friend and ask him or her to first speak while looking at your image on the screen. Then, ask that person to speak while looking at his or her camera lens—whether it's on the phone, laptop, or webcam. The difference is astounding and can have a dramatic effect on how you come across.

So what do you do?

Looking at your viewer has some advantages. You can actually read body language and play off the nonverbal feedback you receive. You can also avoid stepping on your conversation partner's words by waiting to speak if you see he or she is about to say something. But is that worth the cost? That depends on the purpose of your presentation or conversation.

If you are presenting a new idea or concept to your team and it is vital that you get a good read on whether it's being met positively or negatively, then perhaps it is better to blow off eye contact and put the emphasis on noting nonverbal cues from the audience.

If you are being interviewed on Skype for a new position and want to make the best impression on your potential employer, opt for looking into the camera as much as possible. It is perfectly okay to periodically steal a glance at the screen. In normal conversation, we look away every once in awhile. However, spend the majority of the time looking at the lens in order to better connect with your possible hiring manager.

Embrace Your Nervousness

Good storytellers know the value of injecting as much energy into their performance as possible. They're trying to entertain and know they need to emote in order to hold the attention of the audience.

When speaking to a camera, it can be difficult to remember the importance of maintaining your energy level, because you can't play off an audience that isn't there. Consequently, the camera has a tendency to flatten your affect. Your vocal range shrinks. Your expressions become less animated. You can easily take on that "deer in the headlights" look. The fact that most people overestimate their energy level on camera only compounds the problem.

Your secret weapon against this might surprise you: your nerves. Most people get nervous when they perform on camera, but as long as we are not talking about paralyzing fear, that nervousness can actually up your game. Some butterflies in your stomach can help you stay focused and be transformed into a higher energy level on camera that combats the flattening effect of two-dimensional video.

My best newscasts were the ones where I was just a little bit on edge and unsure of what was going to happen next. They usually involved a dynamic situation due to breaking news. I knew I had to be at my best because the script was being written on the spot.

Conversely, my worst newscasts were the ones when I was the most relaxed because it was a boilerplate version of the nightly news. Nothing was breaking, and all of the stories had been filed with plenty of time to spare. On one of those occasions, I remember sitting beside my co-anchor in the middle of a show and hearing him read a 30-second story while I yawned just a few feet away. I wasn't on camera at the time, but I would be very shortly—in front of thousands of people. Luckily, I had been a news anchor for long enough to perform at a relatively high level of skill with ease, so this newscast turned out fine. However, that performance was not one I would have saved for my resume tape because I was just going through the motions. While the average viewer might not have noticed, I certainly did, especially when I compared it to those newscasts where I was fully present.

Use your nervous energy to bring out your "A game." If you're not nervous at all, it could be a sign of a bigger problem: a lack of passion.

And believe me—if you don't seem to care about what you are saying, your audience won't either.

Passion Play

Certain topics can pull the passion out of us easily (like our family, our hobbies, or maybe our favorite sports teams), but how do you exude excitement for compliance training? On the face of it, much of what needs to be conveyed in the corporate world isn't inherently thrilling—important, sure, but probably nothing that will cause goose bumps.

Despite the topical challenges, it is still your job to find a way to grab your audience's attention and keep it. I am not telling you to assume the role of a used car salesman with hyped-up delivery and crazy gesticulating. What I am suggesting is that you identify why your message is important for your audience to hear. What do you need them to know? That is your *passionate purpose*, and it is your mission to make them understand that key takeaway and remember it.

Remember, too, that you are asking a lot of your audience. You are requesting that they drop everything else that they may be or could be doing to watch you perform. If you appear bored by your own performance, they will not be inclined to tune in for long.

Beware of Brain Cramps

When presenting to a camera, you are surrounded by distractions. In a studio environment, they are easy to identify: bright lights, unfamiliar technology, crew members moving around. When the camera is located on your phone or laptop, those distractions can take the form of interruptions by coworkers, noises outside your office or home— even your barking dog. It's very easy to lose your train of thought or experience a brain cramp.

There's no way to avoid these distractions altogether, but one way to lessen their effect on your presentation is by being master of your content. If you know your subject matter inside and out, you won't be as easily derailed by the distractions that are part and parcel of being on camera.

However, even being fully in command of your content doesn't always guarantee success.

DEBATE DEBACLE

Four-term Texas governor Rick Perry was hoping for a breakout performance during the November 9, 2011, debate for the GOP presidential nomination. What he suffered was a brain cramp of rather epic proportions. Allow me to share[1]:

> **Rick Perry:** I will tell you, it is three agencies of government when I get there that are gone. Commerce, Education, and the—what's the third one there? Let's see.
>
> (Laughter and gentle ribbing from other candidates, along with suggestions that the third one would be the EPA.)
>
> **Perry:** EPA, there you go.
>
> (Laughter and applause.)
>
> **Moderator:** Seriously, is the EPA the one you were talking about?
>
> **Perry:** No, sir, no, sir. We were talking about the agencies of government—the EPA needs to be rebuilt. There's no doubt about that.
>
> **Moderator:** But you can't—but you can't name the third one?
>
> **Perry:** The third agency of government I would—I would do away with, Education, the ...
>
> (Someone prompts, "Commerce.")
>
> **Perry:** Commerce and, let's see. I can't. The third one, I can't. Sorry. Oops.

Rick Perry's poll numbers dropped rather dramatically after this gaffe, and he dropped out of the race in January 2012.

What was most surprising about this brain cramp was the content was not new to Rick Perry. It was a standard part of his stump speech. His team (and the candidate himself) probably never conceived of a time when those three agencies wouldn't immediately come to his mind and flow from his tongue. The fact that they did not leads me to my next tip.

Do not set audience expectations that you might not be able to fulfill.

How could Rick Perry have saved himself from embarrassment? He could have said, "There are *several* agencies of government that will be gone" rather than specifically saying "three." He might have listed two and then be pressed for more, but he would have had a better chance at recovery.

Brain cramps love numbers, they love names, and they love specificity. Protect yourself by keeping audience expectations vague.

THE BOTTOM LINE: IT'S NOT ABOUT YOU

As much as we will be focusing on your performance, *you* are actually not nearly as important as *your audience*.

Consider yourself an educator rather than a performer. You have a job to do: to teach them about something that directly impacts them, to tell them something they need to hear or to raise their awareness of an issue or idea that they may not care about yet, but they should.

You play a critical role in that information transfer, and if you focus on doing that well, your level of performance should elevate organically.

It also can be a solid technique to combat performance anxiety, according to Jeffery West, an adjunct drama professor at UNC-Greensboro. "When I teach my kids acting, I try to lead them towards focusing on something besides themselves. It's about wanting to affect something, wanting to change something, wanting to send a message. If you are specifically focused on what you're doing, then you don't have self-consciousness," according to West. "As soon as you start thinking about what your hands are doing, you're screwed."

Enough said.

 Exercise for the Mental Mind-Set

ACTIVITY

This exercise will allow you to test out some of the techniques, which fall under the M of the MVPs of Performance Success. You will be given a scenario, but the actual content to fit that scenario is up to you. However, I would suggest you keep the performance brief—no longer than two minutes. A video longer than two minutes will test the attention span and patience of your viewer.

You will record yourself presenting to a camera, and then review it in whatever playback function you have at your disposal. I will offer guidance on what to look for, like potential performance pitfalls.

If you like what you see, great, but if you see room for improvement, try it again with some tweaks based on your observations.

(*Continued*)

(Continued)

 **WARNING**

Do not flip past this activity (or any other "Exercise" activities you come across in this book). The real learning is in the doing, not the reading. The only way to cement the concepts is to try out the techniques for yourself, so I implore you to give it a go.

WHAT YOU WILL NEED TO COMPLETE THIS EXERCISE

You can use any of the following to record and review your performance:

- Webcam capable of recording to a computer with a playback function
- Smartphone or tablet with the camera app set to selfie video mode
- Laptop with built-in camera video mode (available on most PCs and Macs)
- Camcorder that has an option for reviewing video clips

SCENARIO

Think about something you are passionate about and use that as the basis for your performance. Maybe you want to talk about why you are so devoted to a certain hobby or a particular sports team? Perhaps you want to talk about something that is related to your job or career? The topic itself is not important as long as you have some emotional energy invested in it.

RECORDING YOUR PERFORMANCE

Before you begin your performance, think about your audience and visualize that one viewer. Remember, getting into the proper mental mind-set is crucial.

Consider what you want your viewer to remember and why you want them to care. Don't worry about having a beginning, middle, and end. You just need it to be long enough so you can judge how you are coming across on camera.

Start recording and speak directly into the camera lens. Concentrate on what you are saying, rather than how you are saying it. Once you feel like you have a clip that's long enough to be reviewed, stop recording.

PLAYING IT BACK: HOW TO CRITIQUE YOUR PERFORMANCE

Take a look at the recording of your performance. What did you observe?

If you appeared to be having an animated conversation with an individual, you likely were pretty happy with the results. As you learned earlier in this chapter, an on-camera presentation is more like a conversation across the dinner table rather than a performance on stage.

However, if you were not satisfied with how you performed, allow me to point out some common performance pitfalls.

Wandering Eyes

Forgetting to focus on the audience is one of the most common mistakes I see. The good news is that the "People Pleaser Syndrome" is easy to defeat.

If your eyes seemed to be darting around the room, correct your behavior during take two by forcing yourself to keep a laser focus on the lens. Looking away every once in a while is fine, but primarily, you should be looking at your viewer. Remember, they are looking right at you. Do them the courtesy of returning the favor.

Inner-Critic Hijack

You may have witnessed the "inner-critic hijack," a moment where the conversation coming out of your mouth was joined by a second conversation inside your head between you and your judgmental self. It can manifest itself in a variety of ways. The apparent signs are a grimace, stuttering, or maybe even a muttered profanity. The not-so-apparent signs are a subtle change in facial expression, which makes you look less connected, stiffening of your body, or a bit of rambling while you try to get yourself back on track.

To stave off the hijacking, give yourself some grace when you initially make what you consider a mistake. Viewers are usually very forgiving.

(Continued)

(Continued)

I had a TV news colleague who had a unique way of accomplishing this. Periodically, if he had trouble pronouncing a word, he would gesture as if he was trying to pull something out of his teeth. He'd pry out the offending syllable, to comic effect, and continue with the story. It was certainly authentic to his personality and allowed him to move on both physically and mentally. You don't have to go as far as that, but pushing past a trouble spot is essential to maintaining the integrity of the rest of your performance.

Here's what to attempt on your second try: If you mess up a word, do what you can to correct it quickly, and then continue with the same level of energy and intensity as before. If you keep thinking back to your trip-up, you will cut the quality of the remainder of your performance.

Robo-Presenter

If your performance appeared flat, you likely suffered from "robo-presenter." You may have articulated everything correctly, but you probably were not truly connecting to the meaning behind the words, sounding robotic rather than natural.

Creating a clean take is a "nice to have" but not the goal. The goal is to connect with your audience through authentic delivery. For your second run-through, try not to be so precise in your word choice. Trust yourself to communicate concepts rather than specific sentences. We all somehow manage to make sense in casual conversation without overthinking how we are going to get from the beginning of a sentence to the end.

Remember to focus on *what* you're saying, not how you're saying it.

CHAPTER TAKEAWAYS

- When communicating through a camera, you are always speaking to an audience of one.
- An on-camera conversation is intimate, like speaking across the dinner table rather than from up on stage.
- Visualize a viewer to get in the proper mental mind-set.

- Transform nervousness into energy to combat the flattening effects of video.
- Avoid brain cramps by being master of your content.
- It's not about you—it's about what your audience needs to know.

NOTE

1. Transcribed from YouTube clip at https://www.youtube.com/watch?v=ByGf8lP87HU.

CHAPTER **4**

V—Vocal Variety: Pacing and Pausing with Purpose

n seventh grade, one of my assignments for English class was to write an autobiography that included what I wanted to be when I grew up. I was not able to narrow it down to just one potential career, so I chose two: a news anchor and/or a Broadway star. Somehow along the way, I ended up starting off college as an accounting major, but in my sophomore year, I found my way back to my "true north" and changed my major to communications while continuing to sing wherever and whenever I could.

I started voice lessons in my tween years and continued with them right up to the birth of my second son in my early 30s. Nearly two decades of vocal training have deeply influenced my own delivery as well as how I teach others about how to use their voice effectively while presenting on camera.

THE MUSICALITY OF YOUR DELIVERY—WHAT'S YOUR RANGE?

"Are any of you musicians?"

That's the first thing I ask my class when we start discussing the vocal element of performance success. With my musical background, I am predisposed to think in terms of vocal range, and I know that those who sing or play an instrument will likely speak my same language and have ears attuned to hearing the low and high notes in speech.

As a singer, I boast a fairly wide range: three octaves, which means I can sing all parts from alto to high soprano. When I speak, I tend to also use a wide range of pitches depending on what I'm saying. If I'm excited about something, my pitch will be higher. If I'm delivering something of grave importance, my pitch will be lower.

That variance in pitch is essential in keeping your audience's attention.

What Is Vocal Variety?

In the movie *Ferris Bueller's Day Off*, actor Ben Stein memorably played an economics teacher who famously uttered the words that have become a catchphrase: "Bueller? Bueller?" Stein spoke in such a monotone that his students had to fight off sleep—a fight that some did not win. You could blame the content of the lesson, which was not exactly scintillating, but the steady tone of Stein's delivery sealed the students' fate. The moral of the story: do not be the droning professor.

Research has shown our brains are hardwired to pick up change in our environment and to ignore anything that is predictable, routine, or repetitive. Think about what that means in the context of your delivery: if you speak without changing the pitch of your voice, you risk becoming white noise, and your audience will tune you out.

Vocal variety means allowing yourself to exercise your full vocal range, dipping into the low notes as well as lilting to the high notes of your voice. Everyone's vocal range is unique. Some people have a very wide range, while others have a more narrow range. One is not better than the other—they're just different. What's important is to not confine your voice to one or two notes, relegating your oratory to the equivalent of a lawn mower hum.

Vary your pitch to appropriately reflect your content. If your audience was hoping for a cure for their insomnia, send them elsewhere.

Natural versus On-Camera Inflection

The vast majority of us do not sound like Ben Stein and have at least some vocal variety in our normal conversation, but often that natural inflection is lost once we step in front of a camera. Why is that the case? It gets back to the conflict between concentrating on content versus concentrating on performance.

In casual conversation, a person's natural inflection changes based on what he or she is conveying. Imagine if a mom gave a directive to her children in a monotone. Do you think they'd hear her? Probably not. Instead, she'll probably emphasize the vital information by highlighting certain words: "Please *come here* right *now* or you will end up in *time-out*." (For fun, try to say that in a monotone.)

The natural tendency when you're speaking on camera, especially if you're reading off a teleprompter, is to lose that inflection because you're simply saying the words and not thinking about the meaning *behind* the words. To reclaim your natural inflection, you need to always stay connected to the content and let that serve as automatic pitch control.

SETTING YOUR PACE WITH THE VIEWER IN MIND

Being nervous is not inherently bad when performing on camera, but it can manifest itself in ways that are problematic. One of the more damaging by-products is rushing.

Most people are not thrilled to be on camera and would rather get it over with as quickly as possible, but if your goal is to deliver a memorable message, you will fall short if your speech is like a runaway train that breathlessly pulls into the station.

If you are delivering a performance live, your audience will have only one chance to hear, process, and understand your message. Even if it is a taped performance, you can't rely on their being motivated enough to rewind. Zoning out is a very real possibility.

The average person can speak at a rate of 125 to 175 words per minute but can listen at a rate of up to 450 words per minute. That disparity gives listeners ample time to have their minds wander.[1]

A viewer-friendly pace is measured and deliberate, yet still energetic enough to hold the audience's attention.

While it is not an apples-to-apples comparison, for the sake of illustration, consider a kindergarten classroom. Let's say the teacher is the presenter and the students are the viewers. The teacher wants her class to do three things. Does she quickly spit out directions one, two, and three and expect her class to do what she is asking them to do? Of course not. They can't process all of that information and actually act on it. Instead, she gives step-by-step instructions at a pace appropriate for a classroom of five-year-olds.

I am not advocating that everyone speak like a kindergarten teacher when on camera, but I do recommend keeping the limitations of the viewer in mind at all times. If you are speaking about an especially technical topic, slow down to accommodate the extra processing time your listener will probably require. Conversely, you can likely speed up a bit if your topic is less dense.

The time to be truly deliberate, however, is when delivering any key takeaway. You don't want your viewer to ask, "What did he just say?" On-camera performances usually don't allow for Q&A after the fact. You have one shot to get your point across, so make it count.

FINISHING YOUR THOUGHTS

One of my favorite clips that I use in my workshops features the host of a popular show pitching to a commercial break. Her cohost says his bit and then tosses it to her. She smiles and says, "Well, white, blah blah blah, blake," which produced a look of bemusement and befuddlement from her cohost. What she was most likely *trying* to say was, "Well, right after the break, we will reveal one of the couples who is in the bottom two."

No, she wasn't struck by some medical malady, nor was she terrible at her job. What she had done was "mentally moved on." Her thoughts were already in commercial, but her mouth was still required to form the words to get her there. The result was gibberish.

If you are getting to the end of a performance, you may be elated at the prospect that you are almost done and prematurely mentally check out. However, that moment of anticipation can disrupt your focus ever so slightly that you stumble. Make sure you give each word, each concept, its proper value no matter where it is in your presentation. Maintain your energy, conviction, and focus from the first sentence to the last. Do not relax until the recording light is off.

USING THE POWER OF THE PAUSE

If you are looking for immediate impact on your on-camera performance, look no further than this section. Learning how to employ proper pausing when communicating through the camera can add instant professional polish.

Pause for You

As a classically trained singer, I have been well versed in the value of taking a full breath. Without allocating the time to fill your lungs with air, you will never hit that high C to bring that aria to a spine-tingling close. When preparing a song, you actually identify places to take a breath to create optimal musical phrasing.

The same can be said of speaking on camera, but due to nervousness or a wish to wrap up quickly, many people try to test the limits of their lung capacity by only stopping to breathe when absolutely forced. Unfortunately, the longer you go without taking a breath, the thinner and thinner your sound becomes until finally you have to suck in some oxygen, lest you pass out. Gasp.

Full vocal tone requires you to take full breaths, but the physical benefits don't end there. Deep, even breaths can also be a solid weapon against anxiety. Before any presentation, take some time to breathe through your butterflies a bit. If you breathe through your nose, no one will even notice you are doing it. In addition, research from the human cognitive neuroscience unit at Northumbria University has shown that a shot of oxygen will give you a cognitive boost. Who wouldn't want that before performing on camera?

SILENCE OVER STUPIDITY

CASE STUDY

One of the best pieces of advice I have ever received came during the early years of my broadcast career, from my co-anchor on a morning show. He was about 20 years my senior and was kind enough to share some pearls of wisdom with me, the neophyte beside him on the anchor desk. He told me, "Don't start talking unless you have something to say." The translation: Silence is far preferable to saying something dumb.

In general, we do not like silence. We don't like that empty space and do our best to immediately fill it. Sometimes, we move too quickly and start speaking before a full thought has been formed, which can be a bit of a gamble. Maybe we get lucky and surprise ourselves with our verbal riffing. Maybe we end up babbling into incoherency.

Learn to get comfortable with the silence, and use it to gather your thoughts before leaping into the next sentence or concept.

My stint on the morning show required quite a bit of ad-libbing. The producer wanted friendly banter between his co-anchors, and I did my best to hold up my end of the conversation. Unfortunately, I think I fell short on some days, which likely led my colleague to offer that simple, yet profound, advice.

Remember:

- Don't start talking unless you have something to say.
- Pausing can protect you from sounding less intelligent that you are.

Filler Words as Placeholders

One of the ways . . . uh . . . we try to fill the . . . uh . . . silence is through . . . um . . . filler words. So . . .

Does this sound like you? Perhaps not all the time, but maybe when you haven't prepared as much for an unscripted presentation as you should have and are realizing that fact in real time?

We all use filler words at one time or another, but they can become more prolific when you are delivering a high-stakes presentation, on camera or off. Filler words are a way to momentarily take a mental break while you try to remember what you are going to say next. You may be speaking, but the words you use don't carry any meaning. They are placeholders.

To a viewer, filler words can be incredibly annoying if they are used excessively and can distract from the heart of the message. If your audience is too intent on counting how many times you say "um," they will have a hard time focusing on the actual content. Plus, filler words undercut your credibility, making you sound unsure.

If you know you are a filler-word fiend, try this technique. When you are about to utter your favorite filler word (such as *um, uh,* or *so*), swallow it and substitute silence instead. It'll give you an opportunity to gather your thoughts and carefully consider your word choice, without annoying your audience with a filler word that is the equivalent of verbal drool. If you pause with purpose, you will end up coming across more authoritative and in command than if you opted to simply uh . . . vocally . . . um . . . hang out before your next thought.

Pause for Them

While pausing is valuable for you as the speaker, it is essential for your audience.

Let's go back to the kindergarten class example. That teacher not only slows down her rate of speech (aka pace), she also likely uses pauses to make sure her children are following along. She gives direction number one and makes sure they are following it. Then she gives the next direction and waits for them to accomplish the task. Finally, she gives the last direction and watches them successfully complete it.

It's easy for the kindergarten teacher to know if her pauses are adequate, because she can see her students with her own eyes. But when speaking on camera, you don't have the benefit of being able to visually assess whether your audience is following along. Instead, you have to assume that they are and then allocate the proper amount of time for them to digest your content. In practical terms, that means pausing long enough to let your key ideas sink in, but how long is that?

Earlier in this chapter, you learned that in order to ground yourself in on-camera performance, you need to visualize your viewer. Now let's take that one step further. In order to judge the length of a pause, visualize your viewer's *reaction*. You can imagine them saying, "Oh, I see," or "Okay, I get it." You need to create that silent space as a courtesy to your audience as well as a tool for enhancing your chances that they will remember what you've said.

SILENCE COMMANDS ATTENTION

CASE STUDY

Most people probably admire Jim Collins for his business insights and thought leadership, which he has shared in a series of bestsellers including *Good to Great* and *Built to Last*. I admire Jim Collins for his exceptional ability to employ the power pause.

Collins is a popular speaker who can captivate any audience, whether it's in a boardroom or a stadium. One of his secret weapons, in my opinion, is his use of silence. Collins understands the impact a carefully placed pause can have.

During one of his speeches to an audience at the University of Pittsburgh, he said, "The key to the great leaders that we studied was their (slight pause) humility." And it was here that he pulled off something that I wouldn't try at home—he paused for a full 8.5 seconds. Was it noticeable? Yes. Was it effective? Heck, yeah.

Collins knew that the word *humility* was unexpected, and in order for that surprising statement to have full impact, he needed to give his audience time to contemplate it. He gave them almost 9 seconds to do so—almost forcing them to think deeply about what he had just said.

What was most surprising about that very pregnant pause was the absolute silence that hung there during it. There were no murmurs, no rustling, no squeaking chairs. Jim Collins had his audience right where he wanted them: on the edge of their seats.

That power pause did two things: it allowed one of his key takeaways to resonate, and it built anticipation for what he was going to say next. He said the key was *humility?* What does he mean by humility? His audience wanted an answer, and that pause only heightened their collective desire.

Do we all have the ability to insert 8-second pauses in our presentations? It depends on your performance style. If you are naturally dramatic in your delivery and pause quite a bit in normal conversation, perhaps you can, but the vast majority of us are probably better served by periodic pauses of no more than 3 to 4 seconds. Believe me, a 4-second pause will feel like an eternity to most of us and will provide the same benefits.

Another lesson to be learned from Jim Collins: you can pause vocally but you can't pause your intensity.

When Collins creates that silent space for contemplation and anticipation, he does not use that time to relax. If anything, he intensifies his energy level and connection with his audience through meaningful eye contact, almost challenging audience members to try to look away. Imagine if he simply started ruffling through his notes or checked his watch during that pause—basically forgetting about his audience completely. His audience would have taken their cue from him and also disconnected.

In order to make pauses powerful, you need to maintain your emotional investment in your content. If you appear to be thinking deeply during a pause, your audience will too, and they will anxiously await what you will say next.

THE LOWDOWN ON UPTALK

The 1980s ushered in the age of the Valley Girl and its unusual speech pattern, embodied by a relentless upward inflection at the end of every sentence. The phenomenon came to be known as uptalk or upspeak and seemed to be confined to the ranks of teenage girls from Southern California who turned every sentence into a question.

Fast-forward 30 years, and uptalk has experienced gender and geography creep. While the majority of those who use uptalk tend to be younger and female, the age range has expanded, and men are not immune, according to researchers at the University of California, San Diego.

Through the course of my work, I have coached both men and women who were prone to uptalk. Some of them have been from the C-suite. While it has become less stigmatized due to its widespread adoption, uptalk can still undercut your credibility. If you end every sentence as if you are asking for approval from your audience, you risk sounding unsure and lacking authority.

The Most Common Uptalk Trouble Spot

Most of us do not speak in uptalk on a regular basis, but many of us do have a tendency to slip into it in certain situations. Allow me to address one of the more common trouble spots.

Let's do a quick experiment. Pull out your smartphone and find an app that allows you to record your voice. If you have an iPhone, search for an app called Voice Memo, which comes standard with your phone. Record yourself saying this, "Hello, I'm (state your name) from (where you work or where you live)."

Listen to your recording and take note of your inflection at the end of your name. Did it lift skyward, remain steady, or even drop? If your pitch went up at the end of your name, you have a lot of company. In my classes, this is the most common place where uptalk can be found.

When we introduce ourselves, we may consider it a throwaway line—an obligatory gesture but not one that holds much value. Instead of stating our names clearly and confidently, we have a tendency to vocally lift our pitch as if to indicate there's something more exciting just ahead.

But who you are is an incredibly important piece of information that you want your audience to remember. You will sound infinitely more authoritative if you give your name the proper emphasis it deserves. You may have heard your own name a gazillion times, but it may be totally new to your viewers.

Try recording yourself saying the same line again, but this time, focus on taking your time and dropping your pitch at the end of your name. Consider it an instant credibility boost.

Pausing Practice Exercise

ACTIVITY

This exercise will allow you to practice proper pausing—one of the most effective ways to improve your delivery and infuse your performance with vocal variety. Like the "Mental Mind-Set" exercise in Chapter 3, I will give you a scenario, but the actual content to fit that scenario is up to you. Still keep it around two minutes, so it won't be too burdensome to repeat if you would like to practice multiple times.

As you did before, you will record yourself presenting to a camera and then review it with whatever playback function you have at your disposal. I will again offer guidance on potential performance pitfalls.

Figuring out where to pause and for how long can take some time, so play around with it. Plan your content around a potential power pause moment. Sometimes that can be a provocative question or surprising fact. The real pause pros determine where to insert silence for dramatic effect.

 WARNING

Although I already mentioned this in the "Mental Mind-Set" exercise in the previous chapter, it's worth repeating: Do not flip past this activity, or any other "Exercise" activities in this book. The real learning is in the doing, not the reading. The only way to cement the concepts is to try out the techniques for yourself, so I implore you to give it a go.

WHAT YOU WILL NEED TO COMPLETE THIS EXERCISE

You can use any of the following to record yourself:

- Webcam capable of recording to a computer with a playback function
- Smartphone or tablet set to selfie video mode
- Laptop with built-in camera video mode (available on most PCs and Macs)
- Camcorder that has an option for reviewing video clips

(Continued)

(Continued)

SCENARIO

Think of a story (personal or work-related) that has some emotional heft to it. Practice telling it with purposeful pausing.

- Use at least one pause to create suspense before revealing a key piece of information.
- Pause at least once after delivering a key takeaway.

RECORDING YOUR PERFORMANCE

Before you begin your performance, here's a quick review:

- Remember to get into the proper mental mind-set before you begin your performance. Think about that one viewer on the other side of the lens.
- As you know, vocal variety happens when we focus on the meaning behind our words. Try to stretch to the limits of your vocal range.
- Above all, unleash the power of the pause.

Start recording and speak directly into the camera lens. Once you feel like you have a clip that's long enough to be reviewed, stop recording.

PLAYING IT BACK: HOW TO CRITIQUE YOUR PERFORMANCE?

Take a look at the recording of your performance. What did you observe?

Hopefully, you heard a lot of variation in your pitch that reflected the meaning behind your words. Was your speaking rate appropriate for the tone and level of detail, and did you seem aware of how much information your audience could digest at one time?

How about the placement of your pauses? Did they add value to your performance, or did they seem a little off?

For argument's sake, let's go over a few common performance pitfalls and see if you can identify any in your own work.

Pauses? What Pauses?

While you might have tried to insert pauses throughout your performance, your playback might have told a different story.

Pausing requires us to be comfortable with dead air, something that might not come naturally.

When performing, that two-second stoppage can feel like forever, so we end up shortening our pauses to a length that feels comfortable. Any silence can be deafening to some.

Unfortunately, too short a pause can be so inconsequential that it loses all impact.

On take two, try saying "one thousand one, one thousand two" during a planned pause. You might be surprised how natural that silence seems when played back.

Too Pregnant of a Pause

The flip side of the coin is when the performer tries to pull off a power pause and it simply doesn't fit within his or her performance style.

Jim Collins has a very animated and emotive performance style. Long pauses interspersed with shorter ones seem authentic to his personality and speech pattern.

But you may not be like Jim Collins.

If you watched your video and you felt like your pauses looked contrived, then you need to pause less, shorten the length of your pauses, or both.

Everyone should pause for the many reasons we've discussed, but how much and for how long depend on the individual. This is the time to experiment with what works best for you.

Pausing Your Performance

When you pause in your delivery, you need to guard against pausing your performance. While you may not be talking, you are still communicating, and sometimes the message you send during the silence is off-putting. Pauses can be an opportunity to gather your thoughts, but don't let your audience see you furrow your brow in concentration or stare off camera blankly.

Pauses are also not a time to let loose and relax. That sends the message to your audience that you have temporarily checked out and they can, too.

If your facial expression during your pauses seems off, try this on your next attempt: During your pause, imagine your viewer's reaction to what you just said. It will help you to stay connected to your content and keep your brain from going on a mini vacation.

CHAPTER TAKEAWAYS

■ Vocal variety in your delivery is essential to keep your audience's attention.

■ Recreate natural inflection by focusing more on what you are saying than how you are saying it.

■ Pick your pace with the viewer in mind. Speedy delivery serves no one well.

■ Don't mentally move on. Finish each thought by staying in the moment.

■ Use the power of the pause for you and your viewer.

■ Pauses create an opportunity for you to breathe and collect your thoughts.

■ Pauses allow your audience to digest your content.

■ Silence commands attention.

■ Skip filler words by substituting silence instead.

NOTE

1. R. P. Carver, R. L. Johnson, and H. L. Friedman, "Factor Analysis of the Ability to Comprehend Time-Compressed Speech." Final report for the National Institute for Health. Washington, DC: American Institute for Research, 1970.

CHAPTER 5

P—Physical Factors: On-Camera Movement with Meaning

When we prepare any presentation or performance, we tend to spend the bulk of our time on what we say. However, our words may play only a small role in how well the meaning of our message is understood.

According to Dr. Albert Mehrabian, a research pioneer in nonverbal communication, 55 percent of the meaning of our spoken message is translated nonverbally. Our tone of voice carries an additional 38 percent, while our actual words only convey a paltry 7 percent of the meaning.[1]

Knowing what our body language is saying is crucial, especially if it might be at odds with our oratory. On camera, our bodies speak loud and clear, often without our even realizing it, and that's why it is imperative to understand how to keep our nonverbal communication in sync with our verbal.

ON-CAMERA GESTURING: AN OUT-OF-BODY EXPERIENCE

In the movie *Talledega Nights*, Ricky Bobby, a character played by Will Ferrell, is being interviewed after a race. He asks the reporter, "What do I do with my hands?" He's told to just keep them at his sides. During the course of the interview, though, his hands seem to float into the shot as if they were two foreign bodies with minds of their own.

This was done for comedic effect, but there's a kernel of truth in that bit. When the record light goes on, you can suddenly become hyperaware of your physical self and start asking yourself: *how should I stand, should I stay in one place*, and, of course, *what should I do with my hands?*

Some people choose to simply take their physical selves out of the equation and not move at all. Their heads stay locked in place, and their hands stay in the same position throughout their entire performance—at their sides, behind their back, or in their pockets. But this approach can backfire because the "don't move" technique creates a stiffness that looks uncomfortable to the viewer and surely feels uncomfortable for the speaker.

If authenticity is the key to being effective on camera, then your body language should be the same on camera as it is when you are off camera.

INNER TUBE ARMS

CASE STUDY

While conducting one of my first on-camera performance training workshops, I observed a universal trait of all of my participants that confused me. Every single person kept their arms glued to their sides throughout their entire presentation, as if someone had taken an inner tube and pulled it down over their heads and their shoulders yet stopped short at their wrists. The only gesture that was detectable or even possible was a flick of the hands. However, most kept their palms firmly cemented to their thighs.

During the group analysis of their performances, I commented about the unusual body movement, or lack thereof. I was told they had all taken presentation training and were told that keeping their arms at their sides was a best practice. I am hopeful that they were not instructed to keep their arms there for the entire presentation, but I can't be sure. What I can say is when they tried to apply that principle to their on-camera performances, their arms were super glued for the duration.

HELD CAPTIVE BY THE CAMERA

The camera is not your captor. It is not forcing you to stay still—or even to stay planted in one spot.

I told my class to unglue their arms and instead follow this simple rule: gesture the way you would when you are not on camera. If you like to talk with your hands, then do. If you aren't a big gesticulator, don't feel like you have to create gestures purely for the camera's sake.

Here's the tricky part: most of us are not even aware of how much we gesture. So how do you know where your natural inclinations lie?

Your best bet is to try to have a looseness in your body throughout and allow your gestures to occur organically. The less you think about them, the more likely they will come across as genuine.

I once had a client ask me for a list of gestures to use on camera. I was stymied, mostly because I thought it would be hurting, not helping, his cause. Your presentation style is a combination of your verbal and nonverbal communication, and that style is unique to you. That's why it works. Canned gestures from a list will most likely appear contrived and will make you, the presenter, look fake.

GETTING FAMILIAR WITH FRAME SIZE

While I don't have a list of "Approved On-Camera Gestures," there is one thing that dictates what works and what does not work on camera: frame size.

Frame size, in short, is how much you can see of you and how much you can see of your background in the shot. There are three main categories:

- A tight shot
- A medium shot
- A wide shot

How you are framed changes the closeness of the conversation and thereby changes how big your gestures can be. The wider the shot, the bigger your gestures can be.

Gestures for a Tight Shot

When you are framed in a tight shot, your audience will basically be able to see you from the shoulders up with only a little bit of the background. In essence, you are very close to your viewer and you are having a very intimate conversation.

Think about the kind of gestures you would use with someone in person if he or she were only a few feet away. Would you be throwing your arms wide and gesticulating with gusto? Surely not—it would seem very out of place.

When you are being framed in a tight shot, your gestures need to shrink in size based on the close proximity of your conversation partner or be kept out of the frame completely. Waving or even periodic glimpses of fingers can be distracting, and you want all of the focus to be on your face.

Gestures for a Medium Shot

A medium shot is generally framed from the waist up. Your viewer will be able to see a little bit more of the background than on a tight shot and your arms, when bent, will appear in the frame.

Consider this conversation like a cocktail party. You are close enough not to shout, but you have a little more distance and freedom to gesture and move.

In a medium shot, you still want to avoid giant gestures, which might extend beyond the screen. However, you can feel free to talk with your hands as you would in normal conversation.

A word of caution: Do not allow your arms to play peek-a-boo. Constant bending and extending your elbows with your hands jumping in and out of the shot will draw attention away from what you are saying. While it is totally fine to have your arms both extended naturally as well as bent, just make sure it is not done in rapid succession.

Gestures for a Wide Shot

If you are being framed in a wide shot, you are free to move about the studio—well, not the entire studio, but you can move much more than you can in a tight or medium shot.

In a wide shot, the viewer can see you from head to toe and can also see much of your background. Wide shots aren't used for long periods of time. In a formal studio production, it might be reserved for the opening shot of a video before the director calls for a cut to a tighter shot for the bulk of the production.

When you are being framed wide, you have the freedom to use those big gestures, almost as if you are standing in front of a classroom or a large conference room.

THE GIANT GESTURER

CASE STUDY

When my class participants perform their first on-camera presentations, I usually ask to have them framed in a medium shot. However, I don't let them know about frame size until after they do their baseline records.

During one of these initial performances, a participant told his viewers that he was going to talk about three things, and he used a gesture to emphasize that point. He extended his arm fully and directly into the camera and held up three fingers.

(Continued)

(*Continued*)

As mentioned, the shot was a medium shot but leaning toward a tight shot. You could see his body from about the belly button up, but when his fingers extended toward his audience, the majority of his body disappeared behind them.

Have you ever seen the effect some anglers achieve when they place their relative guppy close to the camera? The fish looks *huge*.

In this presenter's initial video, his fingers looked *huge*, which was not his intention. His gesture might have been fine if the framing was much wider, but the tight framing made his extended hand look like a 3D video gone wrong.

One of the first things to ask when you step in front of a camera is, "How are you framing me?" Not only will you sound like a pro, but you'll also know what to do with your hands—or what *not* to do.

Gestures as a Retention Tool

While the vast majority of your gestures should be natural and not canned, there are times when a planned gesture can add value to your overall impact. Gestures can help your audience retain your content if they complement your words.

Your body language can be a visual aid. For example, if you are talking about revenue rising, you can show it rising by making a vertical gesture with your hand. If you have a broad spectrum of experience, opening your arms wide will serve as a visual representation of that.

A word of caution: make sure your gestures match.

THE MIRROR EFFECT

CASE STUDY

In one of his videos available on his web site, business thought leader Jim Collins talks about what he calls the "Hedgehog Concept" in an animated way. He gesticulates quite a bit and uses his hands to help viewers visualize the main ideas.

At one point, he talks about three circles associated with the Hedgehog Concept and refers to one of them being in the lower left. He then makes a circle with his hands and positions it to what is indeed his left. Unfortunately, to his viewers, that "lower left circle" is actually lower right. He forgot that the camera has the same reversing effect as a mirror.

Collins created cognitive dissonance for his audience by saying one thing and showing another. In order for planned gestures to be effective, they have to support your words, not be at odds with them.

If you are talking about profit growth, your gesture should be vertical, not horizontal. If you are talking about moving east to west, make sure your motion goes from the viewers right to left and not your right to left.

Any conflict between the visual and the verbal could cost you by creating a moment of misunderstanding. You may have moved on, but your audience may still be trying to sort out the mixed message you sent before.

THE ROLE OF *OFF*-CAMERA MOVEMENT

While a tight shot represents a very close, intimate conversation with your viewer, it does not mean all movement must cease. In fact, if you do stay stock still, you will likely appear stiff, uncomfortable, and unconvincing.

Even if your gestures cannot be seen in the shot, they serve a vital purpose. They help you to release tension and allow your words to flow freely. If you are physically relaxed, your delivery will be as well. If your jaw is clenched and your hands are balled up in fists, you will have a very difficult time coming across as confident. A hand movement might not be seen on camera, but it will have ripple effects through your shoulders and be visible to your viewers. Even small motions add visual interest while allowing you to channel some nervous energy outward.

POSTURE POINTERS

The way you stand or sit during a performance plays a central role in your effectiveness on camera and can make an immediate impression—good or bad—on your audience.

Ideally, you will start from a place of comfort, a position in which you feel most at ease yet still energized. Too often, novice speakers are told to stand or sit in a certain way that feels awkward. That advice creates an immediate barrier for the performer. He or she must overcome the challenge of feeling uncomfortable from the get go. Posture is personalized, just like gestures, and should be unique to you.

Standing While on Camera

If you are going to be standing for your performance, use your default stance. If you're not sure what that is, try this: the next time you're having a casual conversation standing up, take note of your posture and how your feet are positioned. Is your weight evenly distributed between both feet? Are you leaning to one side? This is your default stance and should be your go-to position when starting any performance when you are standing up.

The Metronome Effect

If you find you are someone who typically stands with his or her feet parallel with weight evenly distributed, then you should start your performance from that position. However, a quick word of warning: those who stand with feet parallel run the risk of the metronome effect.

It's a common misconception that our feet need to stay rooted in the same spot while on camera, but the performer often feels the impetus to move. That can result in the performer swaying side to side. If the camera is in a fixed position, the presenter can appear to be rocking from one side of the screen to the other, in a rhythmic fashion. Not only can it be distracting, it can also make your viewer seasick.

If you feel yourself starting to sway, try to channel that movement into your gestures rather than full body movement. If you want to avoid the problem altogether, try placing one foot slightly in front of the other. It is nearly impossible to rock side to side.

Going for a Walk

No doubt, you have seen speakers who pace back and forth across the stage when presenting to a live audience in front of them. Movement can be a coping mechanism for nervousness and can help the presenter stay on track with his or her content. On camera, though, pacing will either make your audience dizzy or send you right out of frame.

But that doesn't mean your feet are stuck to the floor. It is perfectly acceptable to shift your weight from one hip to the other. We do it in casual conversation, and we can do it on camera, too. Just be sure the change isn't so dramatic that it sends you careening from one side of the frame to the other. A wide shot will allow for more movement than a tight shot will, so be aware of what your limitations are.

When I teach traditional presentation training, I tell my clients to move to a new position in the performance space when transitioning to a new topic. The same rule applies to shifting your weight. It can be a visual cue to your audience that you are about to introduce something new when you slightly shift your weight.

Sitting While on Camera

Speaking on camera while sitting might seem like an easier scenario to navigate. After all, you don't have to think about finding your default stance, rocking yourself silly, or walking out of frame. However, sitting can pose its challenges, too.

The biggest mistake people make when performing on camera while seated is sitting too far back in the chair. This poses a problem on two levels.

Comfortable chairs can sap your energy. When you relax into a chair, you tend to let down your guard and lose that mental sharpness required for any impactful performance. There's also an aesthetic issue. Sinking into a chair can make you look sloppy on camera. Shirts have a way of bubbling or gaping, the shoulder line of your suit might look uneven, and your clothes overall may appear rumpled.

You want to look sharp and feel sharp. Both are difficult to accomplish when you are lounging.

The solution is to sit erectly with your back either just touching the chair or not touching it at all. By sitting up straight, your clothes should lay the way they are designed to look best. You will also stay better engaged; your body won't be fully at rest, nor will your mind be.

Crossed Legs

Is it appropriate to cross your legs when on camera? This is a question I am asked on a regular basis.

As a young lady, you are often taught to cross your ankles, not your legs at the knee. However, I have always found that advice challenging on camera because form follows function.

When I am performing on camera with a script, I like to keep a hard copy in front of me as a safety net in case the teleprompter fails or adjustments need to be made on the fly. Often, this means I keep my script in my lap. If I keep my legs flat or simply cross my ankles, it is hard for me to glance down at my script without it being noticeable. Crossing my legs at the knee lifts my script high enough that I can refer to it quickly and practically imperceptibly to the audience.

For men, the same rule can apply. However, if you cross your legs with your ankle resting on your knee, be aware that in some cultures, showing the sole of your shoe can be offensive. Make sure the bottom of your shoe is angled away from the camera.

Leaning In or Out

Now that you are aware of the dangers of rocking side to side while presenting on camera, let's discuss what your body language says when you move toward or away from the camera.

Just as Facebook chief operating officer and author Sheryl Sandberg suggests, *leaning in* can be highly effective in the workplace and on camera.

When we are confiding in a friend, we lean toward him or her to signify that we are about to share something important. When speaking on camera, you can use movement toward the lens to invite your audience in and create a deeper connection with your viewer.

One of the more infamous examples of the power of leaning in came in 1995 when CBS anchor Connie Chung conducted an interview with Kathleen Gingrich, the late mother of former House Speaker Newt Gingrich. Chung asked Mrs. Gingrich what her son had told her about then-President Clinton. Mrs. Gingrich said, "Nothing, and I can't tell you what he said about Hillary." Chung encouraged her to reveal what her son had said, but Mrs. Gingrich still balked *until* Chung leaned in and said, "Why don't you just whisper it to me, between you and me?" At that point, Mrs. Gingrich opened up and opened a Pandora's Box. Who knows if Chung's body language made the difference, but on camera, you can see Chung physically lean in toward Mrs. Gingrich. She appeared to be trying to cultivate a deeper level of intimacy with her than might be considered appropriate for an interview to be televised to the masses.[2]

Pushing ill motives aside, movement toward the camera and your viewer can make you come across as earnest and genuine. It helps to build trust between you and your audience, which ultimately builds credibility for your message.

Step In to Start

One of the most confounding moments in any on-camera perfor-mance is the 10 seconds before the red light goes on. All of the stress associated with the high-stakes nature of the presentation is written all over the presenter's face. He or she wears an expression of pained anticipation or frozen fear. The performer is simply staring into the camera lens and waiting to be "on."

A trick to eliminate the nonverbal broadcasting of that anxiety is to use movement prior to the performance. If you will be standing during your presentation, figure out where your mark is. Your mark is the spot where you will be in sharp focus and centered in the frame. If you are working in a studio, you will be told where that spot is, and often a piece of tape is placed on the floor as a visual reminder. Once you are given your mark, stand on it, but then take a step or two back, away from the camera.

Just before you begin your performance, step back up to that mark. When you hit your landing spot, say your first words as you settle yourself into your default stance.

By stepping into the shot, you create movement from the start and avoid the dead stare that so often precedes a performance. It also is a way to invite your audience in because you are closing the gap between you and your viewers.

If you are seated, you obviously can't step toward the camera. However, you can still lean toward the camera and derive the same benefits. Your audience feels welcomed and you are respecting the intimacy of the conversation.

CASE STUDY

BACK OFF BACKING AWAY

One of my trainees came into my class with quite a bit of on-camera experience under her belt. She also was a confident public speaker and carried herself like the former star athlete that she was. Funny and warm in person, I expected she would exude the same on camera, but when she performed, I was surprised that she was missing the latter. The diagnosis of the problem hinged on her body movement away from the camera.

When she spoke, she had a habit of rolling back on her heels and lifting her chin. In person, you wouldn't give it a second thought, but on camera, it came across as arrogant and off-putting, two adjectives that would never be associated with her personality.

To remedy this, I instructed her to focus on moving toward the camera. Moving away from it sends the message that you consider yourself above the viewer, almost as if you are pontificating from on high—not a way to gain your viewer's buy-in or trust.

The small tweak resulted in a total shift in the tone of her nonverbal communication, which allowed her on-camera persona to match her off-camera one.

MAKING EYE CONTACT WHEN YOU CAN'T SEE YOUR AUDIENCE

Any presentation coach will espouse the virtues of good eye contact with your audience, so what do you do when you can't *see* your audience?

The most common practice for the novice is to never, ever take one's eyes away from the camera lens. Imagine if that happened in real life, off camera. You are in conversation with someone and he or she locks eyes with you and absolutely refuses to let you go for minutes at a time. Not only can it be unnerving, but it can also be downright creepy. Nonstop eye contact with the camera is like drilling your gaze into your viewers' heads.

Look Away

Looking away from the lens can feel like an impossible feat, especially if you are reading from a teleprompter, but let's put it in the context of a conversation off camera.

You naturally shift your gaze throughout a conversation, even if it's a subtle glance upward when you are trying to recall a bit of information. Sure, the majority of your time is spent looking into the eyes of the person with whom you are speaking, but that periodic break in eye contact is a welcome one. Otherwise, it would be exhausting for both the speaker and the listener.

According to Carol Kinsey Goman, author of *The Silent Language of Leaders: How Body Language Can Help—or Hurt—How You Lead* (Jossey-Bass, 2011), "Too much eye contact is instinctively felt to be rude, hostile, and condescending; and in a business context, it may also be perceived as a deliberate intent to dominate, intimidate, belittle or make 'the other' feel at a disadvantage."

The argument against staring down your viewer is a forceful one, but how do you pull yourself away?

A break in eye contact can be most effective when associated with a pause. By combining a look away with a pause, it can signal to your audience that you are transitioning to a new concept or that you are gathering your thoughts before proceeding.

However, a word of warning: Breaking eye contact should not be a big gesture. You would be amazed how dramatic a shift in eye line of only a few inches can be. If you are in a formal studio setting, a glance to just below the lens will suffice. If you are using the camera on your phone or laptop, look to the bottom of the device for a half second before looking back at the lens.

Performance Pitfalls: Eye Contact Errors

When breaking eye contact, looking down or up periodically appears most natural, but beware the sideways glance. Looking off to one side every once in a while is fine, but if you make a habit of looking to your left or right too much, you will look unsure of yourself and your content. Plus, your viewer might wonder what you are looking for—is someone coming to get you?

Another no-no is making the eye movement too obvious. A prolonged look away from the camera can cost you the connection you have with your audience. They might think you are done with your presentation and tune out. Breaking eye contact should not require your head to swivel in the direction of your gaze. If it does, the movement will look contrived, manufactured, and out of place—almost as if your attention were diverted somewhere far off camera.

Vary Your Angle

If you absolutely can't pull yourself away from the camera lens, there is another option that will diminish the "deer in the headlights" look. You can change the angle of your head relative to the camera.

Watch one of your recorded performances. If your shoulders stayed square to the camera and your head never moved, you will want to incorporate some variation into how you physically address the camera.

Try loosening up your shoulders and neck and allow your head movement to reflect your content. Be careful not to lift your chin too much to avoid looking pompous. Remember the rule about movement toward the camera. A slight leaning in with your head and a lowering of the chin will create intimacy.

Look Up

When anchoring a newscast, you have several cameras on which you can appear. The director decides which camera to use for each story, and usually there is someone called the floor director, who points to the camera that is "live."

After being burned too many times by being cued to the wrong camera, I took it upon myself to confirm which camera was being used by consulting the monitors embedded in the desk. Right before I started to read the story off the teleprompter, I would look down at the shot and quickly assess what camera was live based on the background. If it was camera three, I would look for the weather set. If it was camera one, I would look for the skyline backdrop. Only then would I look up and start to read the next story.

Looking up at the start of each story was a product of protecting myself from being caught off guard, but it also served as a built-in break in eye contact, which appeared natural.

You learned about the benefits of stepping into the shot at the beginning of a performance. You can also eliminate the awkwardness of anticipation by averting your gaze until a split second before speaking.

Use those few seconds right before you perform to gather your thoughts, visualize your viewer, and channel any nervous energy. You don't need to look into the camera to do that. Instead, look slightly below the camera until you are ready to speak. Then, look up just a beat before saying your first words. That eye movement will signal to your audience that you are ready to engage and will inject more energy into your presentation than if you had spent those moments beforehand just staring into the lens.

ACTIVITY

 Exercise for Frame Size Faults

This exercise will allow you to practice performing within the parameters of different frame sizes. As you learned, you may be presenting while in a tight shot, medium shot, or wide shot. Your freedom of movement is limited by the size of the shot; the wider the shot, the more room you have to gesture and move.

You will be given a scenario, but the content that fits the scenario is your own choice. You will be performing it at least three times, so you will want to keep it brief.

Gather your equipment required for you to record and review your performances. I will raise your awareness about typical trouble spots.

▶ **WARNING**

Yes, I am asking you to do this three times. Yes, it will require an investment of time. Yes, it will be worth it. Please do not skip this part. When you find yourself in a situation where it counts, you will be glad you practiced when it didn't.

WHAT YOU WILL NEED TO COMPLETE THIS EXERCISE

You can use any of the following to record yourself:

- Webcam capable of recording to a computer with a playback function
- Smartphone or tablet with the camera app set to selfie video mode

(Continued)

(*Continued*)

- Laptop with built-in camera video mode (available on most PCs and Macs)
- Camcorder that has option for reviewing video clips

SCENARIO

You have been asked to join a group (work related or hobby oriented) that meets virtually. Introduce yourself to that group by including a greeting along with a description of what you do. Finish by thanking them for the opportunity to join the group.

- **First take:** Stand as far away from the camera as possible to create a wide shot. Introduce yourself.
- **Second take:** Stand closer to the camera so you can see yourself from the waist up. Introduce yourself again.
- **Third take:** Stand or sit close enough to the camera to allow just your shoulders and head to be seen. Introduce yourself for a third time in this tight shot.

RECORDING YOUR PERFORMANCE

In order to create the proper framing, you may need to improvise how to set up your camera if you don't have a tripod. Ideally, you want the camera to be at eye level, which might mean setting up your laptop, tablet, or phone on top of a dresser. Books can also be a low-tech way to adjust your camera position to the proper height.

Think about how the different frame sizes affect your movements. Feel free to experiment to test the limits, so you can see for yourself what works and what does not.

Start recording and speak directly into the camera lens. Review after each take and reset the camera or your position relative to it to create the different framing required.

PLAYING IT BACK: CRITIQUING YOUR PERFORMANCE

Compare and contrast your three different recordings. While the content remained relatively the same, did your gestures change based on the framing?

If you felt that your nonverbal communication was perfectly in line with your verbal, no need to read on. However, if you thought your physical performance could use some polishing, here are a few common problems that you might have observed.

Nonexistent Gestures

Even the most well-intentioned presenters have a tendency to forget to move. If you noticed that your hands played a minimal or even no role in communicating your message, you will want to figure out a way to get them involved.

Presenters who keep their arms down at their sides have difficulty finding a way to bring their hands up. The expanse their hands have to travel to get up to their waists can seem vast, so they opt to just leave them dangling or even behind their backs.

Try keeping your arms bent from the start to get your hands in the ready position to participate. If you choose to clasp your hands together, make sure you don't keep them in a death grip. You want to keep a looseness in your body.

Another option is to start with a gesture toward the camera. It might be extending a palm or opening your arms to the audience, as a gesture of welcome. When you start with movement, it often serves as a catalyst for movement throughout.

Inappropriate Gestures for the Closeness of the Conversation

A wide shot allows for a wealth of gestures, but that is the least used shot when communicating through the camera. Most of the time, you will be either on a medium shot or a tight shot, both of which represent a relatively close conversation.

If you happen to be a heavy gesticulator, you may have found that your hand movements were too big for your framing. On a medium shot, that might translate into gestures that go out of frame. A constant bobbing of your hands in and out can be very distracting. The solution is to rein them in a bit. Stay true to your instincts to move but understand the importance of keeping them relatively contained as you would when talking with someone a few feet away.

In a tight shot, any intrusion by your hands would be inappropriate. The focus needs to stay fully on your face, and fingers in the foreground would draw attention away. Maintain movement but keep any hand motions out of frame.

CHAPTER TAKEAWAYS

- Your gestures on camera should reflect how you gesture off camera provided they are not distracting.
- Frame size dictates how much room you have to move.
- Gestures can be an excellent retention tool but need to match your oratory.
- Movement is essential even if it's off camera to banish the stiff look.
- Begin any performance from a place of comfort.
- Find your default stance.
- Consider stepping into the shot to generate looseness in your body from the start.
- Be careful not to sink into deep chairs, lest you appear sloppy.
- Movement toward the camera is inviting.
- Movement away from the camera comes across as arrogant.
- Attempt to periodically glance away from the camera. Nonstop eye contact creates a death stare for the viewer.

NOTES

1. A. Mehrabian, *Silent Messages: Implicit Communication of Emotions and Attitudes.* Belmont, CA: Wadsworth, 1981 (currently distributed by Albert Mehrabian, am@kaaj .com).
2. This interview is on YouTube as well as at http://themorningspew.com/2012/01/26/connie-chung-interviews-kathleen-gingrich/.

SECTION
THREE

Ready to Wear . . . or Not

For all of the emphasis I have placed on authenticity, that rule does not apply to what you wear on camera. You want your audience to focus on what you are saying, not what you are wearing. Now is not the time to be showing how "on trend" you are or showing off your collection of vintage Hawaiian shirts. On camera, boring is better.

This section covers some wardrobe do's and don'ts, and gives you guidance on how to find a camera-friendly outfit in your own closet. It will also make the pitch for makeup so your performance, not your nose, will shine. The section is divided into the following chapters:

- Chapter 6: Looking the Part—Wardrobe 101
- Chapter 7: Hair and Makeup

CHAPTER **6**

Looking the Part—Wardrobe 101

When I anchored the noon newscast, there were weekly segments during which I interviewed a special guest on a topic aligned with a theme. On Mondays, it was time for "Doctor on Call." Thursdays were reserved for the "Home Pro" or "Pet of the Week." Fridays were the tastiest days of the week, thanks to "Cooking with Class." The segments were not hosted from the anchor desk, but rather from what we called the interview set, which was equipped with the required furniture like a portable kitchen or a puppy playpen.

I am a relatively statuesque gal, nearly six feet tall with seemingly five feet of my height attributed to my legs. Periodically, I would wear skirts to work. While it was not normally an issue, on "Doctor on Call" days, it caused controversy—at least in the eyes of one of my more vocal critics. When standing, my skirts would always hit somewhere just north of the knee—certainly nothing risqué. However, when I would sit down, my skirt would travel a little higher and expose a bit more of my leg—an already genetically elongated expanse, exaggerated by the camera angle.

Had this image not been broadcast, I would not have thought anything of it. But it was, and one particularly persistent caller regularly brought a perceived problem to my attention.

[BRRNGG]

Me: "Thank you for Turning to Ten. This is Karin Reed. How may I help you?"

Female Caller with a Gravelly Voice: "Stop wearing those short skirts. You look like a slut."

Me: "Thank you for your feedback and for Turning to Ten."

My initial thought was, "What level of crazy do you have to hit to actually go out of your way to hurl insults at a person on TV based on the length of her skirt?" My second thought was maybe she was doing me a favor.

What she made me realize was that although your on-camera appearance isn't everything, it is something that you need to pay attention to—even if it's just to make sure the audience isn't distracted by how you look. People notice what you are wearing. But you don't want that to be the focus—you want your message to be. So even if you are the least vain person around, consider it not an act of vanity but awareness that you actually put some thought into your on-camera attire and appearance.

MATCH AUDIENCE EXPECTATIONS

Communicating through the camera allows you to mimic an in-person conversation with anyone, whether they're on the other side of the building or on the other side of the world. As such, you should choose your wardrobe based on what you would wear if you were speaking to an audience in the same room.

As with almost every aspect of on-camera performance, the viewer is your guide. The best rule to follow is to dress to meet the expectations of your audience, which often means reflecting what they will be wearing.

When I am cast as an on-camera spokesperson for a financial institution, the wardrobe they request is usually buttoned-up and formal: a dark suit, blue blouse, and minimal or no jewelry. If I am appearing on camera for a software company, my dress is no fancier than business casual.

Consider your audience and what you would wear if you were meeting them in person. You would not show up at a board meeting with C-level executives in jeans and a T-shirt—unless that's the widely accepted attire of your particular organization. You would also not dress to the nines for a casual conversation with your colleagues.

How you are framed will give you a bit more freedom, though. At my first television station, the sports anchor had a habit of looking polished in his suit and tie from the waist up, but from the waist down, he was beach-bum casual with cargo shorts and flip flops. During a virtual meeting, you can probably get away with pajama pants if you know you will be seen just from the chest up, but what if you need to get out of the chair momentarily to silence your dog? Your striped PJ bottoms might suddenly become a topic of conversation.

As a rule, use the expectations of your viewers as your guide, but not the only guide. On-camera appearances do require some wardrobe adjustments in order to keep the focus on your words and not your clothes.

BORING IS BEST

Often, an opportunity to appear on camera is out of the ordinary and, perhaps, high stakes. Maybe you've been asked to represent the company in a marketing video or you are interviewing for your dream job on Skype. You want to look your best, so you rush out to the store to find the perfect thing to wear. Unfortunately, that shopping trip can fail you when you're drawn to the latest styles and trends.

The best on-camera outfits are timeless and basic. (Some may even call them boring.) This serves a dual purpose. When you are speaking on camera, you don't want anything to distract your audience from your message. A complicated shirt or scarf can take the focus away from what you are saying and shift it to what you are wearing. Wearing something classic can also help extend the shelf life of your video if it's being recorded. If you think your video might be around for a while, you want to remove anything that might date it. (Think giant shoulder pads, ladies.)

SPIN THE COLOR WHEEL

A friend of mine decided to simplify her wardrobe a while back. Her entire closet is now filled with clothes that are all black. Black pants, black sweaters, black jackets. Sure, she might have a contrasting colored blouse or camisole for a pop of color, but those alternatives are few and far between. If she were asked to appear on camera, she would have a distinct challenge because basic black can be complicated for the camera to read.

Cameras have come a long way in their ability to detect detail, but when black is the primary color of your clothing, it can be hard for any camera to tackle. Black clothes can suck all the light out of the shot, and they can also end up looking like one dark blob. Black can be even more problematic if someone who has a light skin tone is wearing it. The camera cannot make sense of the high contrast and overcompensates by throwing off skin color.

Other color no-no's: white and bright reds. Unless you want to appear ethereal, you should avoid wearing white as your primary color. Your white clothes will glow, reflecting way too much light.

Certain reds can also be too vivid for the camera. A tomato red may blow out the color balance on your camera and blow away any chance that your audience will pay attention to your message.

So what colors do work well on camera?

When showing up for a shoot, I always arrive with at least five blouses in an array of colors, but I easily could have brought just one. I hold up the different tops for the producer and, inevitably, he or she chooses this one particular blouse that's a shade of cerulean blue leaning towards turquoise.

Blue is a solid color choice for anyone on camera—pick the shade that you like best. But blue isn't the only color option. Jewel tones can help to liven up the shot and usually play well with most background colors. Some video producers advocate wearing only pastels. However, if you are pale-skinned, you can end up looking washed out.

The majority of us are drawn to colors that complement our complexions and make us feel good when we are wearing them. That will serve you well as you consider what color to wear on camera.

Special Consideration: Green-Screen Shoots

If your on-camera performance is in a formal studio setting, you may be standing in front of what is called a green screen. A green screen is just that: a backdrop that is the shade of a leprechaun's clothing on St. Patrick's Day.

A green screen is used when employing a post-production technique called chroma keying. It allows the editor to lay an image or video on top of anything in a specified color range, green being the most commonly used color to create the effect. This technology trick is used in anything from major motion pictures to television news.

When I began my broadcast career, I started as a weekend weather person. Make no mistake, I was not a meteorologist, but at the time, having a good relationship with the National Weather Service folks and a basic knowledge of high and low pressure systems sufficed. I stood in front of a green screen, a wall of green, with a monitor to my left and right as well as a mirror image of myself in the camera parked in front of me. Through the magic of chroma key, my weather maps were projected on the screen behind me for all of my viewers to see. However, if I physically looked behind me, all I saw was that field of green. I was able to point to the different fronts and meteorological graphics by looking into the monitors that showed the computer-generated maps, with me in front of them. It took some time, but I learned how to interact with the map as if I were staring right at the real thing, not a wall of green.

The first time I ever did the weather, I was horrified to look into the monitor and see myself upside down due to some technical snafu. Not only was I confronted with figuring out my right from left (remember, it's mirrored) but I had to determine it *upside down!* I managed to muddle my way through the weather report, but it was definitely an abbreviated one.

As a weathercaster who always stood in front of a green screen, I knew I could *never* wear green. If I ever did sport a kelly-green blazer, I could end up wearing part of a map of western Pennsylvania on my lapel. Anything in that chroma key color range runs the risk of becoming part of that blank canvas on which other images or video can be superimposed. If you wear a cape of green standing in front of a green screen, you can become a floating head—which is cool for a horror movie but not for your typical on-camera presentation.

Always ask what your background will be. If you will be shooting in front of a green screen, avoid wearing that color at all costs, whether it is a Kermit the Frog shade or teal. If you are wondering if a shirt or jacket will "key out," bring it with you to the shoot and test it out on camera ahead of time. Just be sure to have other options, lest you end up wearing the map of Pennsylvania on your chest.

Solids: A Solid Choice

Let's get back to discussing one of the most important factors when picking your on-camera wardrobe: patterns or the lack thereof.

Solid colors are by far a better choice, because patterns can produce what is called the *moiré effect*, which makes your clothes appear to be perpetually dancing.

According to Nasim Manurov, a professional photographer and founding author of *Photography Life*, "Moiré pattern occurs when a scene or an object that is being photographed contains repetitive details (such as lines, dots, etc.) that exceed the sensor resolution. As a result, the camera produces a strange-looking wavy pattern."[1]

The moiré effect can be produced by a variety of textures and patterns in clothes. Tweeds, small checks, and stripes are always suspect, but even some woven textures in a solid color can dance.

CASE STUDY

ONE HOT BLAZER

The moiré effect image reprinted with permission from Ed Collevecchio.

After two decades in the business, you would think I would not make the newbie mistake of picking an outfit that is not camera friendly. However, I recently opted for a burnt-orange blazer for a professional spokesperson job. While it was not my "go-to" blue shirt, it was close to that category in my on-camera arsenal. I had worn it many, many times for all sorts of on-camera work. Imagine my surprise and distress when I got a phone call from the producer the day after the shoot. The piece had been recorded using two different frame sizes: a tight shot from the shoulders up and a medium shot from the waist up. The blazer looked just fine when the framing was waist up, but all of the takes done in the tight shot showed a very active wiggle all across my jacket. The offending blazer had a distinct weave—a weave that caused no issue for countless performances prior but obviously caused one this time.

Key Learnings:

- The capability of cameras is constantly evolving. The way the technology reacts is not always predictable.
- All solids are not created equal, so if in doubt, bring plenty of options.
- Do a pre-performance check in front of the camera with all the shots being used.

PUTTING ON THE POUNDS

"The camera adds 10 pounds." Fact or fiction?

The answer is full of controversy. Some will say the camera is a truth talker—those extra pounds are all yours. However, another theory is the extra weight is due to a lack of depth perception.

We have two eyes that allow us to view a subject from slightly different angles and assimilate those two shots into a single view. A camera has only "one eye" which can't pick up on the nuances of objects relative to the lens. Consequently, a camera can flatten—and fatten—objects.[2]

What we can agree upon is that the way we dress for the camera can either add pounds or slim us down. Cameras like clean lines, so clothes that are more tailored help us to look trimmer. For example, jackets or shirts that have straight shoulder lines flow smoothly over your physique, and a well-cut suit will make you appear more fit than a shirt that is a little too snug and bulges in places where you'd rather it not.

Conversely, bulky sweaters or pieces without a defined shape can make you look heavier than you are. The camera has a hard time picking out the different layers of the look and detecting where *you* end and your clothes continue.

DRESS RIGHT FOR THE MIC

Inevitably, someone will show up to class in a fabulous sheath dress—tailored with clean lines, no detectable pattern. It seems like a safe choice, especially if it's in a camera-friendly color. Right? Yes and no. It all depends on the microphone you will be using.

In a formal studio setting, audio can be captured primarily in one of two ways: a boom microphone or a wireless microphone worn on the body.

A boom microphone is made up of a directional microphone mounted on a boom arm or pole. It can be held by someone or placed on a stand just out of frame. Boom mics are very popular for both television and film production because they allow freedom of movement for the subject who doesn't have to worry about wearing a microphone.

A wireless lavaliere microphone is the more common option used for corporate video. It can be clipped onto your clothes and is connected to a battery-powered transmitter that sends the audio signal to the receiver on the camera or wherever the sound is being recorded. Lavaliere mics require minimal setup and can be found at all levels of video production.

Pack Placement

Back to the sheath dress . . .

If the video is going to be shot using a boom mic, that gorgeous dress will work just fine, but if you are required to wear a lavaliere microphone, you may have a problem. Not only does the actual microphone need to be clipped on, but the transmitter needs to be clipped on somewhere too.

That sheath dress leaves you few options. You *could* clip the transmitter pack to the back of your dress at the nape of your neck. But the wire that extends from it may make you look like you have an antennae coming out of your head. The other option would be even more indiscreet. (Use your imagination.)

When choosing what to wear, think about where you can clip both the microphone as well as the transmitter pack. A belt around a dress can suffice as long as you are careful to hide the wires and you won't be seen from the back. The safer choice is to wear something with a waistband where the pack can easily be hung.

Microphone Placement

The transmitter pack requires careful consideration, but the lavaliere microphone does as well. Mics vary in size, but all of them work best when being clipped to a stable spot that can stand up to its weight.

The gold standard for mic placement for men is the tie. The microphone can be fastened to the necktie with the cables run behind it, allowing it to be centered and at a proper distance away from the speaker's mouth.

For men and women, jacket lapels also provide perfect places on which mics can reside but can be trickier if the speaker is part of a panel discussion and will be looking to both the left and right. The microphone will not be able to pick up the sound as well when the speaker turns away from it. For that reason, the audio engineer will try to center the microphone as much as possible.

More casual looks should also be chosen with the mic in mind. Anything with a V-neck or buttons down the front is preferable to a high-necked shirt. A jewel neckline may force the microphone to be placed in an awkward angle under the chin, which might muffle the sound.

The fabric of the shirt also plays a role. A silk blouse or a thin sweater may fold under the weight of the microphone, resulting in a rustling sound that may show up right at the end of an otherwise clean take. Opt for a heavier fabric that will maintain its structure when the microphone is clipped on and won't buckle if you move during the course of your performance.

Jewelry Jukebox and Light Show

So you've bought this amazing chunky necklace that you can't wait to show off. Just make sure you're *off* camera when you do.

Necklaces can offend the audio in multiple ways. If they are made up of several strings, they can create sound when they rub together, which can easily be picked up by the microphone. Direct hits can happen, too. A necklace and mic collision cannot be edited out.

Bangle bracelets should also stay in the jewelry box. Their clatter has no place on set.

One unlikely enemy to the on-camera performer is a watch. If you are sitting at a desk and gesturing, you can inadvertently knock your wrist against the tabletop. The microphone can pick up the clank. (The same is true for buttons on the sleeves of some blazers. While you definitely want to gesture, seek to keep your wrists off the desk to avoid creating extraneous sounds.)

Audio issues are not the only interference jewelry can make. Light loves to bounce off metal and other shiny materials. Avoid pieces that may shimmer, glint, or reflect whatever light source you are using. Flashes or sparkling splashes should be reserved for the dance floor, not your video.

Also carefully consider what you adorn your ears with as well. While dangling earrings won't create noise, they can create a visual distraction if they swing about in rhythm to your head movements.

YOUR FIFTH APPENDAGE: A SMARTPHONE

It might seem misplaced to mention smartphones in a chapter on wardrobe. After all, for many of us, our phones are mere extensions of our bodies, and that may be why this rule may be the most difficult one to follow: Keep your phone out of the studio.

The obvious reason: if you forget to silence your cell phone, your personality-driven ringtone will not be appreciated as background music. The less obvious reason: cell phones can create nasty-sounding interference with audio equipment.

Some audio engineers are rather dictatorial on this and will just stop short of patting you down to make sure you did not smuggle one in. This intense scrutiny was required when old cell phone technology did frequently cause hits on the audio in the form of buzzes, blips, or static.

Smartphones and the networks on which they operate have come a long way and no longer cause as many headaches for audio engineers. But you don't want *your* phone to be the one that does. The prudent and often mandated option is to keep your cell phone out of the studio.

Do you really think you will answer a text or phone call in the middle of an on-camera performance anyway?

ADDITIONAL CONSIDERATIONS FOR MEN

Just like the obligatory childhood photo of you missing your two front teeth, there probably is a shot of you wearing clothes that are way too big for you.

Sit on it.
Glenda Powers © 123RF.com

Hopefully, your suit fits you better than this little guy's does, but even today, you too can look like a toddler who raided his dad's closet.

When seated, the collar of your jacket may bunch up in the back, making your shoulders look sloping and your neck look lost. The solution is as low tech as it gets. Pull your suit jacket down and sit on it. Immediately, your shoulder line will be restored and you will appear much more buff than before—all without a trip to the gym. (You're welcome.)

Sock Style

Expressing your personal style through socks may seem like a low-key way to make a fashion statement, but you may be shooting yourself in the foot.

If you are sitting down and happen to cross your legs, your crazy sock style may steal the show and distract your audience from your message. Consider what your goal is. Do you want your audience to remember what you say or what you are wearing? If your follow-up questions center on where you shop, then you'll know what you accomplished.

There is another sock sin that goes beyond distracting style. If you are going to be seated for your performance, make sure your socks are long enough to cover your calf when your legs are bent. A hairy calf poking out between the cuff of your pant leg and the top of your sock is never a good thing.

The Uniform Look

Men have it much easier than women when picking out their on-camera wardrobes. A more formal performance will call for a jacket and tie. A more casual one will require a button down or golf shirt.

Unfortunately, simplicity can create its own problem: *the uniform look.*

Consider this hypothetical: After reading this book, you are asked to participate in an on-camera panel discussion. You grab a blue shirt out of your closet because you have learned the color blue usually plays well on camera. However, your other panelists may have brought their favorite blue shirts to the shoot as well. The result: a panel of blue-clad men looking like they are in full compliance with the company dress code.

Unless you are hoping for a sea of solid color, bring a spectrum of options to help break up the monotony of the "blue man group."

To Button or Not to Button?

That is the question. The answer varies based on whether you are sitting or standing.

If you are sitting, you will almost always want to keep your jacket unbuttoned. Jackets tend to buckle at the button when seated and create a two-fold gape at the chest. In order for the jacket to lie flat, it has to be unbuttoned. The best bet is to adjust it so that it covers the bulk of your chest neatly.

If you are standing, it comes down to what your viewer expects. If your audience leans toward formality, then you'd better button up, but if your audience likely wouldn't be buttoned up in a face-to-face meeting, feel free to keep your jacket open.

CHAPTER TAKEAWAYS

- Your wardrobe should match audience expectations and reflect what they would likely be wearing.
- Boring is best—solids, no patterns.
- Avoid black, white, and red as primary outfit colors.
- Don't wear any shade in the green family if you are shooting in front of a green screen.
- Consider where the microphone and transmitter pack can be worn.
- Wear clothes that can withstand the weight of the audio equipment.
- Choose your jewelry carefully to avoid audio interference and visual distractions.
- Keep your cell phone out of the studio.
- If you are appearing on a panel, bring wardrobe options to avoid the uniform look.

NOTES

1. To read Nasim Mansurov's article in its entirety, visit https://photographylife.com/what-is-moire.
2. Paraphrased from the article "Do Cameras Really Add 10 Pounds" by Matt Soniak, ©2016 Mental Floss Inc. http://mentalfloss.com/article/31895/do-cameras-really-add-10-pounds.

CHAPTER **7**

Hair and Makeup

For my first TV job, I had the unusual and good fortune of having my parents within my station's viewing audience. They were able to watch their daughter fumble her way through the steep learning curve of her trade.

I will never forget calling my mom after I anchored my first newscast. Here's a close facsimile of the conversation:

Me: Mom, how did I do?

Mom: Oh, Karin, your hair looked great!

Me: Mom, no one cares about my hair.

I was hoping for a glowing critique of my anchoring skills. The assessment of my hairdo was not what I was expecting. I thought it was totally inconsequential. How wrong I was.

Many years and a TV station later, I had my "eureka" moment. On a whim, I decided to chop off my long hair into a short, modified pixie style. When I went on the air that night, the phones lit up at the station. It seemed everyone wanted to weigh in on my new 'do. In fact, I was told by the station operator that she couldn't recall another time when the phones were busier. Thankfully, the comments were mostly positive, but it was an eye-opener, for sure.

You may not give a whit about whether your mane is managed, and you may never go near a makeup counter—but messy hair and a washed-out face may not give you the credibility boost you are looking

On-camera classic

90

for. Your lack of interest in hair and makeup could actually diminish the impact of your performance if your viewers can't stop wondering if you bothered to look in the mirror beforehand. Vanity is not the driver—your mission is. Don't let your message be lost in your bangs over your eyes.

HAIR HASSLES

To commemorate one of my anniversaries at my TV station, my colleagues put together a montage of all of my different hairstyles through the years. Of course, the results were a little horrifying. What I thought was cutting edge at the time looked terribly out of touch only a few years later. However, there was a common thread through all of my evolving looks; each style was camera friendly.

I realize you likely did not pick your style based on whether it would flatter your face while on camera. While you may not be able to change your cut for your occasional video appearance, you may need to mitigate potential problems.

Female newscasters were often accused of wearing "helmet head" hairstyles, which seemed to form a shell, similar to the plastic hair caps that can pop on and off of Lego characters. Mockery aside, those styles did serve a purpose. No one sporting one of those hairdos ever had their hair fall over their faces.

If your long locks have a laissez-faire attitude, you run the risk of having them invade your face and appear to swallow it on camera. While it may not be annoying to casually flip it away from your face when talking to someone in person, the repetitive movement on camera quickly wears out its welcome. If you are being shot shoulders up, imagine how exaggerated that motion would appear.

Hairstyles that frame the face can also cause problems. Most studio shoots involve multiple lights, not just a spotlight shining at you from the front. If you are being lit from the side, your hair can cast unwanted and unflattering shadows on your face. Additional lighting can help compensate for it but can't always eliminate it.

Hair problems can also extend to audio issues if your hair extends beyond your shoulders. Lavaliere microphones are the most commonly used mics in corporate video. If your hair is long enough, it can inadvertently brush against that microphone. You may think your hair isn't heavy enough to actually make noise, but often, mics are sensitive enough to pick it up.

So what do you do if your hairstyle is not of the helmet head variety?

If your length allows, consider pulling your hair back to avoid any potential problems. Eye contact is incredibly important in creating that connection with your audience, and you don't want your hair to get in the way of that. Another option is to simply keep your hair behind your shoulders provided it won't stray to the front in mid-performance. If your bangs are the issue, find a hairspray that will keep them in check and away from your eyes.

Hairspray can also be your best weapon when combatting flyaways. Blondes have more of a challenge than brunettes because the light has a tendency to play off the lighter strands. Make sure you have someone check in whatever monitor you are using for stray hairs sticking out in the wrong direction. Harness them with a hairspray that promises a flexible hold or use a smoothing serum to keep the flyaways grounded.

ON-CAMERA MAKEUP MUSTS FOR WOMEN

When working as on-camera talent for a corporate video job, I often have access to a professional makeup artist on site. It may not be quite equivalent to a trip to the spa, but it is purely decadent to sit down in a chair and have someone "fix me." I have worked with countless talented makeup professionals over the years, and I am always grateful for their ability to transform me from a barefaced, sleep-deprived mom into someone who is broadcast worthy.

However, not every camera shoot garners a makeup artist's magic, especially if that on-camera communication is taking place at home over WebEx. (Wouldn't that be fun, though, if every virtual video meeting came with a "makeup artist on call"?)

In the event that you are left to your own devices—and makeup kit—this section gives you some general guidelines to follow that are well within your skills set. You may not be as camera perfect as you would be at the hands of a professional, but you will certainly look camera pretty-darn-good.

WHAT YOU NEED IN YOUR KIT

You do not need to look like a member of the cast of Cirque du Soleil, but you do not want to be washed out. Women who never wear makeup might be uncomfortable with anything on their face, whereas other women who wear it every day may have no problem putting even more on. Finding the amount of makeup that makes you feel and look your best on camera might require some trial and error.

With that in mind, this section describes the *must do's* as well as some *could do's* if you are so inclined.

Moisturizer

Even if you do wear makeup regularly, any on-camera makeup requires a slightly heavier hand. With that in mind, you need to prepare your skin for what is going to be applied. Peeling, dry skin will flake even more once products are put on, so be sure to moisturize in advance. You want to make sure it has time to sink in.

Another thing you can do is apply a primer to your clean, moisturized face. This will create a smooth canvas and extend the life of your foundation.

Foundation

Foundation can create the effect of a smooth, uniform complexion and cover up any minor imperfections. Typically, a liquid foundation will be more forgiving than a full powder one, which has a tendency to settle in wrinkles or fine lines.

Some makeup artists insist upon using spray-on foundation that requires a laborious process you definitely don't want to try at home. Most of you will apply your foundation using a sponge, a brush, or even your fingers. Remember, foundation isn't just for your face. Make sure your neck is covered as well so you don't have an obvious line at your jawline where the foundation ends. If your hands will be in the shot, consider applying foundation to the back of them as well, especially if their tone will be in stark contrast to that of your face.

Powder

Shine is the enemy for any on-camera performer. What may look dewy and youthful in person can come across as just plain greasy on video. Powder, either loose or compact, can take that shine out of the equation. If you are in a studio, you also may sweat under the lights. In fact, if you are doing a high-stakes presentation on camera, you may sweat regardless of the heat generated by your lighting. Perspiration can slide your makeup off of your face. Powder can help to prevent that.

Eye Makeup

One of the first things my students notice when reviewing their baseline recordings is how their eyes seem to disappear. The camera flattens your features. With that in mind, it is up to you to draw them out, sometimes literally.

Simple eye shadow without a shimmer or sheen helps to emphasize your eyes. You don't need to figure out how to create "the smoky eye" or master where to use all three shades in your eye shadow compact, but some color will add dimension that a naked eye does not have on camera. A good mascara and eyeliner will also go a long way toward defining your eyes. Most of the makeup artists I know apply extra eyeliner toward the outer edges of the eye and put a darker shade of shadow in the crease to create a sense of depth.

Your color choice follows the same rule as your wardrobe. Use the color palette that you are drawn to but don't seek to make a statement. You still want the focus to be on what you are saying rather than that crazy shade you put on your eyelids.

The cardinal rule, though, is to opt for matte over glimmer. Santa can have a twinkle in his eye. You should not, if it's the result of some odd interaction between the lights and your glitzy eye shadow.

Cheeks

Through the miracle of foundation, you have created a flawless face, but there's a problem. Your face likely has no definition. Blush can alleviate your apparent lack of cheekbones on camera and adds some welcome color to your monochrome complexion. You will need to apply more than you think reasonable because the lights will blast out much of the color anyway.

Lip Color

While I wouldn't suggest going Marilyn Monroe red, adding color to your lips can also help you define your features. A lip stain or matte lipstick can provide that pop of color but you want to avoid lip glosses, which will reflect the light in unpredictable ways. If you already wear lipstick, there really isn't a need to stray from your norm. If you don't, find a neutral color that doesn't take you too far out of your comfort zone.

MAKEUP FOR MEN

Makeup makes most men squirm. They fear the application as well as the end result. But you want your *performance* to shine, not your face.

When I worked in television news, I had the pleasure of interviewing an entertaining and eloquent mayor named Buddy Cianci. Mayor Cianci went about running the city of Providence wearing a face full of foundation every day. I swear I never saw him without makeup until his mug shot (but that's another story). Buddy made a lot of news, so he was frequently featured on camera. Consequently, he was always camera ready. Buddy understood that his audience would not be able to focus on his words if they couldn't get past his appearance.

I am not suggesting you carry pancake makeup with you at all times, but if you have a tendency to look a little oily, you will want to address it. That could mean using a little powder on the typical trouble spots called the T-zone: the forehead, nose, and chin.

Another option, which might be more palatable, is a clear matte gel found at most makeup counters. It is designed to control shine like a powder but does not add any color. I use one made by MAC Cosmetics on many of my male students, especially those who have foreheads that seem to extend all the way to the back of their heads. You can apply the gel with a makeup sponge, and no one even knows you are wearing it.

Aside from controlling the shine, men are in the low-maintenance makeup category. In other words, you can leave the false eyelashes at home.

GLASSES OR NO GLASSES

One of the most dramatic changes I have seen one of my participants make over the course of training is to go from glasses to contacts. The first day, she watched her bespectacled-self doing her baseline performance and apparently decided she needed to take immediate action. The second session was only two days later, but she came in sans glasses.

Despite that example, going on camera does not mandate that you toss your eyewear, especially if you need them desperately to see.

Deciding on whether or not to wear your glasses is another scenario where form follows function. If you are nearsighted and the camera appears to be a fuzzy blob, you should definitely opt to wear them. If you opt out, you will find it terribly difficult to stay relaxed, because you've made yourself uncomfortable at your core. Even worse, you will squint at your audience.

If glasses are part of your authentic self, then they should be part of your on-camera wardrobe. However, you may have to compensate for a glare from the lights.

Be sure you check out how your lenses interact with the light in the environment prior to your performance. If you are presenting to a camera on your phone or laptop, check the shot beforehand to see if you are registering any odd glares. It may be a matter of adjusting the position of a lamp or closing blinds on the window. If you are presenting in a formal studio setting, ask the crew to watch out for strange reflections. In one of the studios where I often teach, glasses have a tendency to display a greenish cast, which requires some modifications and experimentation with different lighting setups.

If your glasses are simply for style or only for reading, you may want to skip them altogether to avoid any of the issues mentioned.

CHAPTER TAKEAWAYS

- If you do not pay attention to your hair and makeup, you may diminish the impact of your performance.
- Keep your hair away from your face to avoid it becoming a distraction.
- Long hair can brush against the microphone and interfere with a lavaliere microphone.
- Makeup is essential for both men and women.
- Women need a heavier hand when applying makeup for on-camera.
- Men need to keep the shine on their faces or heads at bay by using powder or a matte gel designed to control shine.
- Be aware of potential glare on the lenses of glasses and adjust the lighting if necessary.

Best Practices for Creating Your On-Camera Message

How you construct your content can be just as important as how you perform it. Whether you are working off a script or speaking extemporaneously, what you say should be shaped by the medium through which you are communicating.

This section focuses on techniques for structuring your content for the spoken word so your message is heard and retained. It offers guidance on organizing for the ear as well as best practices for writing a script that will sing, not force you to perform verbal jujitsu. The section is divided into the following chapters:

- Chapter 8: Organizing for the Ear
- Chapter 9: Writing for the Spoken Word

Organizing for the Ear

Humans are terrible listeners. That simple fact should serve as your primary guide for how much information you try to convey in a presentation on camera.

Don't just take my word for it. Consider research done at Babson College, which looked into how much information an audience can retain after watching television news. On average, viewers who just watched and listened to the evening news could only recall 17.2 percent of the content when not cued, and the cued group never exceeded 25 percent.[1]

You may want to include every single detail you can about your topic. After all, you want your viewers to get their money's worth. However, just like drinking from a fire hose can't quench your thirst, too much information can easily turn into information overload.

If you can only expect your audience to retain 25 percent of what you say (and that's on a good day), you need to draw their attention to what you want them to remember most. You can do this by giving your viewers a mental framework in which to categorize your content. Organizing for the ear makes it easier for your audience to pick out and retain the most valuable takeaways.

THE RULE OF THREE

One of the oldest tricks for increasing the odds that your audience will remember what you've said is to follow the Rule of Three. This technique has its roots in Aristotle's *Rhetoric* but has been adopted, adapted, and applied to everything from advertising to standup comedy. Its power is based on pattern and capacity.

It boils down to this: Humans process information in patterns. From birth, it's how we try to make sense of the world in which we live. What is the smallest number to make a pattern? Three. Humans also have a cap on how much information they can take in at one time. By using a fierce filter to weed out extraneous content, we end up with a concise, clear message. These two factors lead to this communication equation:

$$\text{Pattern} + \text{Brevity} = \text{Memorable Content}$$

Think about how we memorize phone numbers (when we don't cede the job to our smartphones). Do we try to remember 10, unrelated digits?

8-6-3-6-2-2-6-3-6-4

No, we chunk them into three groups: two sets of three numbers and one set of four.

(863) 622-6364

Examples of the Rule of Three dominate our history and surround us today.

"Veni, vidi, vici." [I came. I saw. I conquered.]

Julius Caesar

"Life, liberty, and the pursuit of happiness."

United States Declaration of Independence

"Government of the people, by the people, for the people."

Gettysburg Address

"Mind, body, and spirit."

New Age mantra

"Location, location, location."

Lord Harold Samuel

The Rule of Three has a rhythm so often replicated that its use is barely even noticeable—except from the pulpit of my childhood church. My minister was a master of the Rule of Three. Each sermon always had three distinct points, which helped to cement the key learnings from that week's scripture. That consistent structure, week to week, also set expectations that the mental framework would be filled in for the congregation before the organist piped in before the benediction.

Applying the Rule of Three On Camera

While the Rule of Three is effective in any presentation, it can be even more valuable when applied to any on-camera communication scenario. Messages delivered through a lens need to be concise and clear. The Rule of Three promotes both.

It simply requires you to think in triplicate.

Rule of Three via Skype

Say you are preparing for a job interview over Skype. You may be tempted to include every single thing about your employment history, education, and skill set. However, we know when communicating through the camera, less truly is more.

The Rule of Three requires you to identify *three* main points that you want to convey. So prior to your interview, try to develop your talking points in triads. Come up with a list of likely interview questions, and choose three pieces of information you want to include in the answer. The Rule of Three can provide an informal framework that can harness your urge to ramble. Once you've articulated your trio of talking points, start wrapping up. Overanswering can have diminishing returns.

MY RULE OF THREE

CASE STUDY

Let me explain with a real-world example. When I am asked, "What do you do?" this is my response:

> "I'm a communication coach. I conduct on-camera performance training, traditional presentation training, and professional development workshops on the soft skills of effective communication."

My three points are:

- ▪ On-camera performance training
- ▪ Traditional presentation training
- ▪ Professional development workshops

This is a very basic version of what I do, but I recognize that I need to create mental buckets for my audience. They're not looking for a deep dive into the finer points of my communication curriculum, but they do want to have a general understanding of what I can provide.

I could tell them all about how I conduct training in group settings as well as one-on-one sessions. I could tell them about my three-pronged approach to presentation excellence. I could tell them about my client list, even citing specific examples. Heck, this could be an hour-long monologue. But they'd remember very little of it.

My goal is to pique their interest and have them come away with a basic awareness of what services I provide. If they want to know more, they will ask after they digest my initial burst of information.

VERBAL DROOL

Alex was the president of a prominent business incubator, but he suffered from his own version of verbal drool. When anyone asked him what the incubator did, he found it nearly impossible to break it down and instead opted to include as much as he could to try to add clarity. His approach had the opposite effect, of course. The more he tried to explain, the more confusing the answer became.

We worked together to strip away the complexity and developed a list of three key talking points, which concisely described what the incubator provides in its own unique way. The process itself was enlightening because it forced him to examine what role he hoped the incubator would play in the start-up community.

Alex had the opportunity to give the Rule of Three a test run during an on-camera interview a short time later. Two minutes of TV time is an eternity, so his ramblings would never have been sound bite friendly. Thanks to the Rule of Three, he was able to hit the highlights with confidence and none of them ended up on the cutting room floor.

Your Core Message

In the "My Rule of Three" sidebar, you may have noticed that I began the explanation of what I do with the following sentence before launching into my three points: "I'm a communication coach." This phrase is what I call the *core message*.

Your core message can best be described as the one thing you would want your audience to remember above all else. It's the most critical bit of information you want them to retain.

While we started the discussion of organizing for the ear by focusing on the Rule of Three, the core message is where you should begin any presentation prep. This preeminent takeaway guides your application of the Rule of Three. Once you have identified the core concept you want to relay, you can better select the proper points to support it.

In the "My Rule of Three" example, I want to emphasize that I am a communication coach. The three supporting points are specific services I provide under the communication coach umbrella. While the core message can stand alone, the supporting points provide context.

The Rule of Three Expanded

By ascribing to the Rule of Three, you have given yourself a universal tool for crafting any presentation, on camera or off, but it can also be built out, if time allows.

If you are doing a longer presentation, you can add subpoints under each of your main supporting points, but continue to think in threes. It would something look like this:

Core Message
- Supporting Point 1
  - Subpoint 1
  - Subpoint 2
  - Subpoint 3
- Supporting Point 2
  - Subpoint 1
  - Subpoint 2
  - Subpoint 3
- Supporting Point 3
  - Subpoint 1
  - Subpoint 2
  - Subpoint 3

By expanding the Rule of Three in tiers, it allows you to build up or scale back your content based on how much time you are allotted.

Let's say you prepared a five-minute on-camera presentation, but you are told you only have two minutes. You could just chop your content from the bottom up, potentially leaving off part of Supporting Point 2 and all of Supporting Point 3.

How about this alternative editing choice? Leave your three main supporting points intact but eliminate a level of detail. Think about cutting vertically, rather than horizontally. It enables you to stream-line your content but maintain the integrity of your message.

REPETITION, REPETITION, REPETITION

When presenting on camera, it is up to you to draw your audience's ears to what is most important. One of the more effective ways to do this is redundancy.

You may have heard this presentation training cliché:

1. Tell them what you are going to tell them.
2. Tell them.
3. Tell them what you just told them.

This may be cliché, but that's because it works.

The majority of people are primarily visual learners, so any communication on camera puts the audience at a distinct disadvantage. There often is no text, just your face. They are forced to rely on their auditory processing almost exclusively. With repetition, you give your audience three opportunities to process your key takeaways: at the beginning, in the middle, and at the end.

By previewing what you are going to say early on, you put your audience on notice to listen for these points. You create a mental outline for them to categorize your content into bite-sized, memorable chunks.

The next step is to fill in that outline by speaking to those points *in the order in which you previewed them*. Why is the proper order so important? You don't want to create any cognitive dissonance. If you told them you were going to tell them what you had for breakfast, what you had for lunch, and what you had for supper, do not start with your lunch menu. You would be leaving a big blank space in the mental outline you have created, diminishing the value of building it in the first place. If you create an expectation, fill it, but in the order you previewed.

Once you've covered your three points, take the time to repeat them one last time as you wrap up to reinforce your key takeaways. If you think you are wasting your time repeating yourself, think back to what the research tells us. We need all the help we can get with retention. And perhaps the third time is the charm?

CHAPTER TAKEAWAYS

- Organize for the ear to combat the deficits in human listening abilities.
- Follow the Rule of Three:
  - Humans process information in patterns.
  - Three is the smallest number to create a pattern.
  - Pattern + Brevity = Memorable Content
- Use repetition to highlight the key takeaways:
  1. Tell your audience what you are going to tell them.
  2. Tell them.
  3. Tell them what you just told them.

NOTE

1. J. Stauffer, R. Frost, and W. Rybolt, "The Attention Factor in Recalling Network News." *Journal of Communication* 33 (1): 29–37.

CHAPTER 9

Writing for the Spoken Word

I f you go into a TV newsroom, chances are, you would see a bunch of people talking to themselves. No, they haven't lost their minds, at least most of the time. What they're doing is writing—out loud.

Anything a broadcast journalist writes is intended to be read aloud, so any reporter or anchor worth his or her salt approaches a script by following this rule:

Write the way you speak.

THE CHALLENGES OF READING WRITTEN PROSE ALOUD

Most prose is intended to never be heard. Instead, it is meant to be read silently—consumed, comprehended, and committed to memory without ever being spoken word for word.

Stylistically, the majority of us have never had to consider how challenging it might be to verbalize our writing. A writer's focus, understandably, is on communicating his or her message in full. If a sentence is three lines long, it's not a problem as long as it follows the proper rules of grammar and includes all the information the writer wishes to convey. It *is* a problem, however, if someone has to try to say that sentence out loud and can barely make it to the end without gasping for air.

As a moderator of webcasts, the most challenging part of my job is the introduction of the esteemed panelists. Often, they come from academia and have the requisite litany of degrees, achievements, and awards. Their bios read as if they were lifted from their institutions' web sites, which they usually are. Few, if any, are reworked for readability. Consequently, the person charged with delivering those bios on camera is forced to perform verbal gymnastics worthy of Olympic gold. (Insert a pat on the back for me!)

Almost all business communication follows the same pattern. How something sounds when read out loud plays no role in word choice, but when that same prose is repurposed for on-camera, the real issue comes to light. While your internal voice is able to glide over almost any conglomeration of words, your audible voice may get tripped up on even the most familiar ones.

In my classes, I often use a stock script with the word *integral*. Everyone in the class knows the definition of the word and perhaps might even use it in his or her own writing. However, someone always stumbles over it when he or she reads this word off the teleprompter.

 NOTE

For those of you who are not familiar with teleprompters, here's a quick definition: A teleprompter is a device that allows the script to be projected in front of the camera. The presenter appears to be looking into the lens while he or she reads the scrolling words.

The problem usually stems from the fact that there are two acceptable ways to pronounce it: in-TEH-gral and IN-teh-gral. The brain has to make a split-second decision on which pronunciation to use, and if it's not a word you say often, there can be a processing delay that results in a noticeable verbal trip—a mangled pronunciation or a very pregnant pause.

The only way to find out where the potential trouble spots are is to actually give full voice to the copy.

WHY THE WHISPER TEST WON'T WORK

The first thing I ask my students to do after I pass out a training script in class is to read it aloud. The next thing that happens is the room erupts into a breathy, low-level hum as everyone starts to whisper their way through the copy. Unless you are planning to whisper on camera, this does you no good. A whisper allows for a multitude of sins: a quicker pace, lazy pronunciation, and a lack of pauses.

A script needs to be easy on the ear and comfortable to the tongue. The only way to find out if that's the case is to read it the way you will perform it on camera.

WRITING TIP 1: KEEP IT SHORT

Run-on sentences are a no-no in any grammar class, and they are when crafting a script for the camera, too. However, the reasons why you want to avoid them may differ.

Long sentences in on-camera copy create massive delivery challenges. First of all, there's a physiological one. A period provides a natural break for you to stop and take a breath. If you have to wait too long for that visual cue, your vocal tone may thin as the available oxygen expels from your body.

Second, you can easily lose your viewer when you take too long to connect the dots. Introducing your subject and then adding layer upon layer of descriptive phrases after that asks too much of your audience. By the time you get to the end of the sentence, they may have forgotten what it was even about.

Third, you run the risk of getting lost in the teleprompter because the end of a sentence is nowhere in sight. An uninterrupted string of words can be tough to follow visually. Punctuation helps to break the copy up into manageable sections.

WRITING TIP 2: DON'T FEAR THE GRAMMAR POLICE

Think back to your language arts classes. You probably remember a heavy emphasis on grammar, punctuation, and prescribed formats for each writing scenario, whether it was a persuasive essay or analysis. You didn't dare have an unclear antecedent, not to mention the horrors of ending a sentence in a preposition.

However, when we speak, our word choice and syntax seldom reflect the formal rules of grammar and structure. And since authenticity is paramount in on-camera performance success, you need to give yourself freedom to speak authentically. So instead of seeking to speak more carefully when appearing on camera, you should seek to match your writing style with your conversational style.

Everyone has his or her own style of speech. Some of us are more formal, while others of us are more colloquial in our word choice. The important thing is to be true to *you*. If you write in your own voice, it will be easier to speak what you write.

My performance style is relatively relaxed, so I tend to use contractions whenever possible. For example, if a script says "I have," I almost automatically convert it to "I've" when I perform it. However, I have had clients who would never contract anything because that would have felt uncomfortable to them. They never use contractions in normal conversation, so doing so on camera would feel contrived.

Let your personal speech pattern dictate your tone, but know that no one is going to call the Grammar Police on you if you end a sentence in a preposition.

WRITING TIP 3: SEE SPOT . . . BE BORED

The *Fun with Dick and Jane* books of the 1950s and 1960s provided countless children a smooth path to reading. But they weren't exactly page turners. The simple structure of the sentences that followed a predictable pattern made it easy on new readers but did not make for scintillating text.

Variety in your delivery is essential in order to keep your audience's attention. It is much harder to have that vocal variation when your sentences all follow the same cadence. ("Sally sees Spot. Spot sees Sally.")

A steady drumbeat of fact, fact, fact can cause your audience's eyes to glaze over. One sentence starts to blend into another and the meaning behind the words becomes lost.

Give yourself something to play with vocally by changing up your sentence structure and intent. Plan power pause moments and employ them. The idea is to indirectly engage your audience by making them think about what you're saying.

Here are a few ideas:

- Ask a rhetorical question. Your audience will start to ponder their answer.
  Example: "What if today was your last day on Earth? What would you do?"
- Offer a surprising fact. You want to create that moment when your audience says, "Huh?"
  Example: "Bill Clinton sent only two e-mails during his presidency: one to our troops in the Adriatic, and one to John Glenn when he was 77 years old in outer space."[1]

EXERCISES FOR WRITING THE WAY YOU SPEAK

No matter how simple it sounds, writing the way you speak can be challenging the first time, second time and perhaps many more times. But once you get the hang of it, it can transform how you approach any on-camera performance.

You will perform two exercises to test out the technique.

ACTIVITY

▼ Exercise 1: Revising Existing Copy

In this first exercise, you will practice rewriting existing copy.

What You Will Need to Complete This Exercise

- Your written bio
- A smartphone with voice recording capabilities; for example:
  - iPhone: The Voice Memo app has been built in since iOS 3.
  - Android: Many voice recording apps are available on Google Play.

STEP 1

Find a written version of your bio. It could be from your company web site, your LinkedIn profile, or your resume. Once you've got your bio in hand, do the following:

1. Record yourself reading it.
2. Play it back and listen for any performance problems.
3. Take note of and mark the trouble spots. For example:
   - Did you stumble?
   - Did you pronounce something incorrectly?
   - Did you run out of breath?

STEP 2

Once you have identified where you tripped up, rewrite the bio in a reader-friendly form, as follows:

- Move through the copy one sentence at a time, editing as you go to make it easier to perform.
- As you write, speak your script out loud.
- Keep editing until you no longer have hiccups delivering it.

STEP 3

Once you have rewritten the bio to your satisfaction, record yourself reading the new version. Then play it back and note the ease with which you deliver the modified version. What changed? Were the sentences shorter? Did you take words out or change them if you found them difficult to say?

It is important that you understand your own particular delivery challenges. You will more readily recognize red flags when you see them in future prose.

ACTIVITY

Exercise 2: Creating New Copy by Speaking Your Script

In this second exercise, you'll create a script by speaking it.

WHAT YOU WILL NEED TO COMPLETE THIS EXERCISE

This exercise requires you to have a smartphone with dictation capabilities. For example:

- iPhone: Use the voice recorder in the Notes app.
- Android: Use Google Keep found in Google Play.

INSTRUCTIONS

This time, try to build your bio from the ground up by speaking your script. Follow these steps:

1. Identify the main themes in your formal bio: your current position, your educational background, any awards or recognition you've received, and whatever else might be germane.
   Write down the key elements in bullet form and use them for reference.

2. Open the dictation app on your smartphone and do a quick test run to ensure it translates correctly and you are speaking loudly enough.

3. Using your smartphone dictation app, record yourself delivering your bio in first person ("I am ..." rather than "*Your name* is ..."). The copy will appear as you say it.

(Continued)

(Continued)

4. Go back and reread your copy out loud and note how it sounds and feels. Is it easy on the ear and comfortable to the tongue?

5. If the dictated version is a bit too rough, feel free to smooth out the edges, but don't sanitize it to the point where you lose your authentic voice.

SIDE NOTE: DICTATION ON LAPTOPS

An author friend of mine told me he wrote his entire book by speaking it into a dictation application. He claimed it made the process much faster and allowed the words to flow freely.

If dictating a script onto the written page works well for you, most Mac and PC operating systems do have speech recognition capabilities. While you can use the internal microphone built into your laptop, you may instead want to use an external microphone that plugs in via a USB in order to improve the accuracy of the dictation software.

On a Mac, the Mountain Lion OS X and beyond have the dictation tool in System Preferences. Once you enable it and set it up, you can use it anywhere you type text. Microsoft Word for Mac actually has a Start Dictation option in the Edit menu. You just have to be sure to speak your punctuation.

Most Windows operating systems also have speech-recognition software built in. It allows you to control your computer with your voice as well as dictate text. To set up this feature, search for **speech recognition** in the Start menu and then follow the onscreen instructions. Just as with the Mac version, you can dictate rather than type any text. Remember to actually speak the punctuation such as "period" and "comma," or your passage may look like you are emulating T. S. Eliot.

CHAPTER TAKEAWAYS

- Write the way you speak.
- The whisper test does not work. Speak your script in full voice.
- Write in short sentences.

- Do not be a slave to the rules of grammar.
- Vary sentence structure and plan power pause moments.
- Dictation software can help you to write the way you speak by taking the typed text out of the equation.

NOTE

1. Adam Clark, "Bill Clinton Sent Emails While President—2 of Them!" *Salon*, February 17, 2011. http://www.salon.com/2011/02/17/bill_clinton_2_emails_president/.

How to Read without Sounding Like You Are

Despite all of my years of schooling, the majority of my work involves something I learned to do in kindergarten: read.

My secret weapon, though, is I am pretty adept at not *sounding* like I'm reading when I am. This is not something I learned in kindergarten—in fact, it's not something most people ever learn at all.

Thankfully, I received some good coaching early on, and I've added my own plays to the playbook over the years to make them my own. In this section, I will open up that playbook for you, and let you in on the tricks perfected over two decades of reading on camera. The section is divided into the following chapters:

- Chapter 10: Marking Your Script
- Chapter 11: Tackling the Teleprompter

Marking Your Script

began my broadcast news career before I could even legally drink. When I was 20 years old and still in college, I was hired, despite my lack of experience, to be the weekend reporter and "weather person" at the local CBS affiliate in Youngstown, Ohio. How could this incredibly green news reporter even maintain a modicum of credibility?

In all honesty, I did at least look older than I was and could project confidence beyond my years. I also knew enough to dress the part, having spent quite a bit of time observing the wardrobes of news anchors at stations where I had interned in the past.

But my voice belied my youth. Undeterred, my news director was kind and savvy enough to conduct an intervention—he hired someone to vocally shape and "age" my delivery. Enter Dr. Candice M. Coleman.

Dr. Coleman holds degrees in speech and theatre and, in the early 1990s, held my career in her very capable hands. Over the course of several months, my St. Louis–based vocal coach became my phone pal, teaching me how to improve my vocal tone with proper breathing techniques for a richer sound. But perhaps the most impactful thing she taught me was how to draw out the meaning of the sentence based on proper emphasis and phrasing. These techniques are based on a book written by Nedra Newkirk Lamar and the Institute of Analytical Reading called *Giving the Sense: How to Read Aloud with Meaning*, first published in 1949 as *How to Speak the Written Word*.

Dr. Coleman worked directly with Lamar back in the 1970s and explains the underlying premise in this way, "Analytical Reading is based on logical principles and conversational patterns that underlie normal speech. Analytical Reading brings out the meaning with the logic."

Even though the concept of Analytical Reading has been around for decades, its applicability is evergreen and can be used by anyone who reads aloud for a living or only on occasion. Ms. Lamar's method became the basis for the Institute of Analytical Reading. On its web site (www.analyticalreading.org), you can find a list of teachers certified in the technique (including Dr. Candice M. Coleman). It continues to be an effective resource for newscasters, ministers, lecturers, and the like.

To this day, I use those techniques along with others I have added over the years to help me read, but not *sound* like I'm reading. In this chapter, I reveal the steps you can take to break down the copy so your delivery sounds natural, not affected.

IMPORTANT CAVEAT

I fully admit I am not a certified analytical reading teacher. I learned the foundational techniques more than two decades ago. This chapter is not intended to serve as a substitute for training by an Analytical Reading coach.

I offer you some general rules I learned and modified based on my own experience on camera. However, if you would like to take a deeper dive into the Analytical Reading method, I encourage you to visit www.analyticalreading.org to find a certified instructor.

STEP ONE: SMOOTH OUT THE SCRIPT

Reading the script out loud at a normal volume should always be your first step, whether you have written the script yourself or someone else wrote it. Actually, if someone else wrote the copy, you *really* need to read it out loud because it will most likely not be written in your style.

Remember, a script needs to be easy on the ear and comfortable to the tongue. If it sounds odd to you, it will probably sound odd to your audience. Rework it. If you trip over a word, change it; otherwise, you will either trip over it again or be so worried about messing that word up that you'll trip over another one close by.

I once was moderating a panel discussion featuring a professor from Penn State. Her name was unusual: Dr. Breffni Noone. I obviously couldn't change it, but I was concerned I was going to screw it up. I practiced saying it aloud several times prior to the broadcast, hoping it would help my mouth to wrap around it more readily. Luckily, it did during the actual show, but unfortunately, I messed up the word *Pennsylvania* a few words after that. I couldn't believe I messed up the pronunciation of my own home state—which brings me to step two.

STEP TWO: ADD PHONETICS WHERE APPROPRIATE

In my ideal on-camera performance world, everyone would be named "Bob Smith"—that pronunciation is as straightforward as it gets. However, since this probably won't ever be the case, I've learned to rely on phonetics. According to Merriam-Webster, phonetics is "the system of speech sounds of a language or group of languages." In the context of this chapter, it's a way to visually write out the way a word sounds.

Let's go back to my previous challenge: Dr. Breffni Noone. Despite my worry about pronouncing it correctly, I had no problem saying it on air, only to mess up an easy word due to my hyperfocus on the troublesome name. What I *should* have done was written the name phonetically like this: BREFF-nee NOON. By writing the name out the way it sounds, my brain would have had less to process. I wouldn't have had that moment of delay, wondering, "How was it pronounced again?"

On camera, the fewer things you have to worry about, the better. You're already in a challenging situation, right?

While my phonetic spellings are definitely not textbook, they are recognizable to me. And that's all that matters. I encourage you to figure out what works for you.

I suggest that you do two things. First, figure out how to write the sounds in a way that you will immediately understand. You don't want to actually make it worse by using a phonetic spelling that you can't decipher. Second, make sure you use capital letters on the stressed syllable.

When I do voice-over work, I sometimes receive a script with a list of phonetic spellings for words that are uncommon or technical, or proper nouns with company-specific pronunciations. Often, those phonetics will not reference what syllable needs to be emphasized. That's like having a map without road names.

Without indicating emphasis, you are giving your brain one more processing task. Make it easy on yourself and provide the map with highways, secondary roads, and points of interest that are well marked.

▋ EPIC OSCAR FLUB

CASE STUDY

The greatest argument for customizing your own phonetic spellings can be based on one of the all-time best mispronunciations, made by none other than Vinnie Barbarino himself, John Travolta.

During the Oscars in 2014, Travolta was asked to introduce Idina Menzel, who was going to perform the Oscar-nominated song "Let It Go" from the movie *Frozen*. The producers knew Idina's name was not in the "Bob Smith" category, so they wanted to help John out by writing it phonetically. Unfortunately, they did so without consulting him. In fact, he was told the name would be written phonetically in the prompter only seconds before he took the stage.

When asked about his epic flub on *Jimmy Kimmel Live*, this is what Travolta told the host: "So I go out there and I get to her thing and I go 'hm?' And in my mind I'm going, 'what is that name?'"

What came out his mouth—spelled using my own phonetics—would look something like this: "a-DELL duh-ZEEM." This set into motion a social media stream of mockery and a series of late-night skits, mocking the muff.

Did John Travolta truly not know the correct way to pronounce her name? Of course not. However, in the moment, he was not able to reconcile what he saw on the teleprompter screen with the right way to say Idina Menzel's name.

Moral of the story: make sure your phonetics are helpful, not hurtful.

STEP THREE: MARK WITH MEANING

Once your script is edited and phonetics are inserted where appropriate, you begin to apply the most basic tenet of analytical reading: marking for meaning.

According to Nedra Newkirk Lamar, "The whole secret of meaningful, and therefore, natural, emphasis lies in stressing the word that carries the thought, the meaning word that gives the sense."[1]

In normal conversation, we naturally stress the words that matter most in a sentence. Otherwise, we would sound bizarre. Let me give you an example. Read this sentence out loud:

I would love to go to the movies.

In natural conversation, you would probably say it like this (the words to emphasize are in bold):

*I would **love** to go to the **movies**.*

Maybe you might put a slight emphasis on the word *go*, but that's probably about it. Now try reading it aloud with this emphasis:

*I **would** love **to** go to **the** movies.*

Sounds weird, right? But why?

In the first rendition, the words in bold were the "meaning words." Even if you took all the other words away, you would still know what the sentence was about: love, go, movies. In fact, in caveman talk, you would actually be able to pull that off as a sentence: "Love go movies [*grunt*]."

Contrast that with the second sentence, where I placed the emphasis differently. If you strip away all of the words not in bold, you are left with: would, to, the. Your caveman sentence would not make any sense at all: "Would to the." None of the emphasized words were essential to the meaning.

The words you emphasize should carry the critical essence of the idea you are trying to present.

 NOTE FOR EMPHASIS EXAMPLES AND EXERCISES

Often, your ear is an excellent guide as to what should be emphasized and what should not. With that in mind, keep your smartphone handy so you can record yourself saying these sentences and then be able to play them back.

If you are conflicted about where the emphasis should be placed, try reading the sentences a few times with different words in bold. Nine times out of 10, you will be able to discern what delivery sounds most natural after hearing it played back.

New vs. Old

Another underlying tenet of Analytical Reading, as taught to me by Dr. Coleman, is the need to emphasize the new idea in each sentence and subdue what has already been introduced.

Senator Bob Dole had an annoying habit of speaking of himself in third-person all of the time—"Bob Dole doesn't like (this) and Bob Dole doesn't like (that)." He would naturally stress his name each time, which made him sound affected and perhaps a bit egocentric, too. After all, we knew he was talking about himself. Why did he keep reminding us?

When figuring out what to emphasize and what to not, think about the Bob Dole scenario. Has your viewer already heard you say this particular word and has already registered its meaning? If so, then don't emphasize it. However, if are you saying something new *about* it, then the new concept relating to it should be what you stress.

Let's build on the previous example:

*I would **love** to **go** to the **movies**.*

What if you added a second sentence? (It may not be factually correct, but just go with it for the sake of the exercise.)

I would love to go to the movies. The last movie I saw was Forrest Gump.

What do you think you should emphasize in the second sentence? The answer to that question requires you to ask yourself two other questions:

- What's the new idea?
- What's critical to the meaning of the sentence?

In the first sentence, you introduced the idea of the movies, so *movie* would not be the meaning word in the second sentence. But what about *last*? That would be new, as would the actual title, *Forrest Gump*.

My suggested emphasis would look like this:

*I would **love** to **go** to the **movies**. The **last** movie I saw was **Forrest Gump**.*

Read it aloud. Does it sound natural to your ears? Let's convert it to caveman talk: "Love go movies. Last "Forrest Gump." Do those words contain the critical information necessary for your audience to understand your message?

Now let's experiment with an alternative reading. Try speaking the sentences aloud with the indicated emphasis in bold.

*I would **love** to **go** to the **movies**. The last movie **I** saw was **Forrest Gump**.*

Did the switch in emphasis change the meaning? Did you perhaps sound a bit sarcastic, as if you were mocking how behind the times you were in your movie-viewing habits? The tone shifted based on your extra emphasis on *I*. If that was the intent, then emphasizing the *I* would be absolutely appropriate. If it was not, then you would have inadvertently added a level of snarkiness simply through misplaced emphasis.

Always make sure your emphasis reflects the meaning first. Sometimes that may even overrule the conversational style.

The Name Stress Principle

Let's try another example together. Read this sentence out loud:

> The Declaration of Independence states that "all men are created equal."

What would you emphasize? Consider what is critical to the meaning of the sentence. You might be overwhelmed because there are so many words that seem valuable. That's true, but if you emphasize too many words, you will diminish the impact of emphasizing any at all. Too much stress can be just as damaging as none at all.

Based on the principles of emphasizing the "meaning words" I would suggest this:

> The Declaration of **Independence** states that "**all** men are created **equal**."

You may ask why you wouldn't stress the entire phrase *Declaration of Independence*. Even though those three words represent one entity, it would be difficult and unnatural to emphasize all of those words. This scenario falls into a conversational pattern called *name stress*.

Dr. Coleman explains:

> When we talk, we'll generally stress the last name of a person or entity—Candy **Coleman**, Robert Lewis **Stevenson**, United States of **America**. When the last word of a multiword entity is generic, we'll usually stress the word immediately preceding it—Columbia **Broadcasting** System, Eveready **Battery** Company.

Based on this principle, simply stressing *Independence* will help you inject that natural inflection into your delivery. Try it for yourself. Doesn't it sound more conversational to just stress *Independence*?

When I've used this example in training, I have had students argue vociferously for stressing *created*. However, stressing two words in a row can be vocally challenging and sound contrived. Consequently, the advocates for *created* were then forced to subdue *equal*. Try emphasizing *created* and listen to the effect.

*The Declaration of **Independence** states that "**all** men are **created** equal."*

This may sound fine to your ears, but consider the caveman translation: "(Declaration of Independence) all *created*." Created what? The word *equal* seems more meaningful and doesn't leave questions in the minds of the listeners.

Now let's add a sentence:

*The Declaration of **Independence** states that "**all** men are created **equal**."*
But it wasn't until 1920 that women were allowed to vote.

What are the new ideas present in the second sentence, which should be brought out by extra emphasis? Resist the urge to stress too many words. I'll allow you three in the second sentence, so think about the words that are essential to the meaning. Here's my suggestion:

*The Declaration of **Independence** states that "**all** men are created **equal**."*
*But it wasn't until **1920** that **women** were allowed to **vote**.*

Caveman translation: "(Declaration of Independence) all equal. 1920 women vote." An argument can be made for "allowed," but you venture into "overemphasis" territory. The other words are all toss-aways in terms of meaning.

How to Mark Your Copy for Emphasis

Thus far, I have marked the words to be emphasized in bold. If you are typing your text, that is one way to mark your script for stress. However, sometimes you will be handed hard copy and be asked to read it off of the written page. What do you do?

When I was given my scripts for a news broadcast, I would immediately start wading through the copy, underlining the words I wanted to emphasize. It's a practice I continue to this day when I am asked to present on camera or off.

The underlined words jump off the page, breaking up the sea of copy. I can even see at a glance when important words are coming up. The visual cues help me to modulate my delivery so I'm not peaking too soon in a sentence. For me, underlined words are mile markers that keep me on track and let me know when I arrive at my destination.

I will address how to adapt these markings for teleprompter copy in the next chapter.

Emphasis Obstacles

Marking for emphasis is not an exact science. There is certainly some variation in what sounds natural for one person yet completely awkward for another.

Following is a brief discussion of two common emphasis obstacles: connotations and too much stress.

Beware of Connotations

Simple shifts in emphasis can result in a dramatic difference in connotation if we are not careful in selecting what we stress.

A client of mine had written the phrase *slightly useful* in her script. As I listened to her deliver it, I sensed there was something wrong but couldn't figure it out right away. After some analysis, I realized her emphasis was misplaced. Here's how she said it:

*They found it **slightly** useful.*

Read it out loud for yourself, and you'll notice that although my client had intended to say something positive about her product, the connotation sounded negative. The wording is a bit awkward because she was reporting on survey results. "Slightly useful" was one of the responses, so she could not change it.

Now try saying it this way:

*They found it slightly **useful**.*

By shifting the stress to "useful," the negative connotation is replaced by a positive one.

It can be very tempting to always stress words ending in -ly (like truly, really, actually, etc.). Sometimes, such words do carry the meaning and should be stressed, but often they precede the word that should be emphasized.

When thinking of the connotation, it helps to look at what Dr. Coleman calls the implied contrast. When you choose a word to stress, often you intend to draw attention to the fact that it is *not* something else. Sometimes the contrast is overt: I would like the *blue* shirt, not the *black* one. However, sometimes the contrast is left unsaid.

Dr. Coleman further explains:

> *When you stress a word, make sure the implied contrast brings out the meaning you intend. Using the term Italian professor, let's see what the implications might be. If you stress **professor**, aren't you implying a contrast with an Italian doctor or engineer or some other profession? Or, if you stress **Italian** aren't you indicating that this professor is from Italy or teaches Italian rather than some other country or language?*

Here's another example. If you are a buying steak at the meat counter at the grocery store, the butcher will ask you which one you would like. You might say you would like the *third* steak from the left. The implied contrast is you do not want the first or second. However, if you would say, "I would like the third *steak* from the left," the implied contrast would indicate you wanted a steak rather than chicken or fish.

When selecting emphasis, be sure to mark for meaning and be aware of the problems it can create when you don't.

Too Much Stress

One of the most difficult tasks for many is to figure out what words are critical and deserving of emphasis. Consequently, the most common pitfall is emphasizing too many words.

If the goal is to draw attention to what matters most through careful selection, by stressing almost everything, you are back at square one. Not only does this defeat the purpose of the exercise, but it also will be painful to listen to.

Always err on the side of underlining too few words versus too many.

STEP FOUR: PLACE YOUR PAUSES

Pausing throughout your performance can give you the professional polish you are seeking. But when you are sitting in front of a camera, silence can be deafening to the speaker—something you should avoid at all costs. A visual cue can be a saving grace for those who can't seem to stop themselves.

Pauses, as you learned, can be highly effective tools for creating suspense and dramatic flair. They can also be essential for your audience to digest what you are saying.

When considering where to employ those pauses, think about what purpose you want each pause to serve. I separate my pauses into two categories: the short pause and the power pause.

The Short Pause

The short pause is designed to separate ideas and concepts—an opportunity for you, the speaker, to catch your breath and an opportunity for your viewer to catch up.

Sometimes, punctuation provides a clue. Pausing at a period or comma is often appropriate, but don't be fooled into thinking it is always that simple. For example, consider this sentence:

In critiques of Broadway productions by my sister, a musical theater composer, Lin-Manuel Miranda is given high marks.

What does *musical theatre composer* need to be related to, my sister or Lin-Manuel Miranda? If you pause at both commas, it is unclear because both my sister and Lin-Manuel Miranda are musical theater composers. However, by vocally linking *my sister* and a *musical theater composer*, isn't the sentence clearer? Also, from a grammatical standpoint, if a *musical theater composer* was supposed to go with Lin-Manuel Miranda, wouldn't there be a comma after his name?

In this case, I would read it as follows:

In critiques of Broadway productions by my sister, a musical theater composer, [pause] Lin-Manuel Miranda is given high marks.

When you run into a sentence with little or no punctuation, you may still need to pause both to breathe and for meaning. Make sure you connect those ideas that belong together and then take the pause. Breaking up words that are all related to each other with a pause can be confusing for the listener. Lamar calls this "What Does It Modify or Belong With?"[2]

The Power Pause

Power pauses can be one of the most effective performance tools in your toolbox, but they may require some forethought to maximize their impact. A power pause, by my definition, is one where the silence does either of the following:

- Builds anticipation for what will be said next
- Creates space for the audience to revel in a revelation

In order for a power pause to achieve the desired dramatic flourish, it needs to be longer than a short pause you take to simply catch a quick breath. Whereas a short pause may be less than a half second, you may be able to say "one-thousand one, one-thousand two" silently during a power pause.

POWER PAUSE MASTER

CASE STUDY

Remember Jim Collins, the business guru and pause master? He demonstrated mastery of both instances in one sentence during a speech he made at the University of Pittsburgh. Here's what he said:

> "The key to the great leaders that we studied was their *[short pause]* humility. . . . *[eight-second pause, which feels like an eternity]* But it was humility of a very special type. . . . It was what I would describe as an absolute burning, compulsive ambition *[three-second pause]* that wasn't about them."
>
> *Source:* https://www.youtube.com/watch?v=q-KyQ90XByY

Here, Collins employed two power pauses for two different purposes.

His first power pause—after *humility*—was designed to create space for the audience to consider what he just said, to contemplate his revelation that the greatest leaders were humble. He gave his audience time to think about that pretty unconventional idea. If he had just breezed from that bombshell to the next sentence, the line would have lost its impact.

His second power pause—after *ambition*—served a different purpose: it created suspense. He delivered the first half of the sentence with intensity and passion, and just as he was about to bring it to its climax . . . he paused. And his audience was right there with him, waiting with baited breath for what he was about to say next.

I imagine that those power pause moments did not happen by chance, but rather were planned in advance. Collins is a pro and probably does not have to mark those moments in his script. However, for us mere mortals, it is advisable to do so.

Marking Your Pauses

How you mark your pauses is also based on personal preference. If you have the luxury of typing them out ahead of time, you might like to use slash (/) for a short pause or a double slash (//) for a power pause.

However, I am partial to ellipses . . . because it seems somehow . . . more natural to me.

Some folks are happiest with a dash to indicate a place to pause— but it all depends on what works for you. Feel free to experiment until you find the one that fits.

If you are forced to mark up a written page of hard copy, your best bet is to use a slash with a flourish of your pencil, not a pen. It's hard to erase a pen mark if you happen to make a mistake. It does break up the text into manageable segments that will help guide your eye and your brain through the performance.

Pause Practice Example

Still a little unsure of what pauses are appropriate? Here's an example I used in my training when *Big Data* was the buzz phrase of the day:

> *It seems like everyone is talking about Big Data, but is there really power in Big Data or is it all just hype?*

In terms of stress, I'll cut to the chase. Despite some variation, here are the most popular word choices for emphasis:

> *It seems like **everyone** is talking about **Big Data**, but is there really **power** in Big Data or is it all just **hype**?*

You might want to do a small emphasis on *talking* as well, but the other words do not carry enough weight to warrant being vocally stressed.

Let's move on to placing your pauses. There are a couple of places where short pauses would seem natural, but there is also an opportunity for a power pause. Are any startling revelations being said or places where the speaker might want to build anticipation?

Here's a bit of context: assume the person saying this works in the software space, specifically in data analytics. Would the idea of this person potentially bashing his livelihood be surprising? Probably, so what about marking pauses in this way:

> *It seems like* **everyone** *is talking about* **Big Data**, [short pause] *but is there really* **power** *in Big Data* [short pause] *or is it all just* **hype?** [power pause]

I even envision a bolt of lightning and a clap of thunder after that statement. What? He called it *"hype??!!"* Assume that the power pause is followed by an elaboration on why that is not the case, but the power pause served a key purpose. It caught everyone's attention and increased the likelihood that they would listen intently to what was going to be said next.

It would be perfectly fine for the on-camera presenter to read this sentence without dramatic pauses, but it would be a missed opportunity to make an impression on the audience.

Pause Pitfalls

As with emphasis, there is such a thing as too much of a good thing. If someone inserts too many pauses into their performance, they can sound affected, unnatural, and downright annoying.

Author Teddy Wayne derided what he called "NPR voice" in an article he wrote for the *New York Times* in the "Fashion and Style" section on October 24, 2015. He described a style of delivery heard in many a podcast (including my personal favorite *This American Life*) where "the speaker generously employs pauses and, particularly at the end of sentences, emphatic inflection." He postulated that the pauses were meant to imitate spontaneous speech but were carefully planned. Rather than praising it, though, he called the style of speech "counterfeit."

To that point, it all comes back to the idea of authenticity. If your communication style leans toward the dramatic, you may be able to pull off more pauses than someone who is more subdued in normal conversation. Do not go too far out of your comfort zone simply because you think it's "what you are supposed to do." If your excess pauses make you feel like a lawn mower struggling to catch, trust your gut, and take some of those pauses out.

It All Comes Down to This . . .

What you stress and where you pause really depends on you and your personal performance style. Some performers can pause for eight seconds and have the audience eating out of their hands, while others look like they are having a mini-stroke.

Use your ears to guide you. If it feels or sounds odd to pause, then don't do it.

ACTIVITY

Extra Emphasis and Pausing Practice

Figuring out how to mark your script can take some time, but the more you practice the techniques, the easier it becomes until it is almost second nature. Rarely, do I have to read every single line out loud to recognize what will trip me up. I know enough now to be able to identify trouble spots at a glance.

But I've been doing it for more than 20 years, and I'm assuming this is new to you. That's why I am including some additional passages for you to analyze on your own. They were not written for the spoken word, so they may not roll mellifluously from your mouth. However, they will allow you to stretch those marking muscles.

You will find an answer key at the end of the chapter. If you placed your pauses and emphasis differently than I did, that's fine as long as you can justify the reasons behind your choices. You may have a style that alters how much and where you pause. You may want to stress certain words that at first blush don't appear to carry the meaning, but for your purposes, they do.

While there are many right choices for pausing and emphasizing, there are also some definite wrong choices. If you opt to emphasize a word that doesn't help your audience understand the meaning of your message, you probably made a bad choice. If you are not pausing at all because you feel like you are drowning in the silence, you likely need to rethink that.

Remember, your goal is to deliver a memorable message. If you just blow through it without drawing out the meaning for your audience, you probably will fall short of that goal.

Sample Sentences

1. "Either the well was very deep or she fell very slowly, for she had plenty of time as she went down to look about her and to wonder what was going to happen next."

   (Excerpt from *Alice's Adventures in Wonderland* by Lewis Carroll)

2. "All children, except one, grow up. They soon know that they will grow up, and the way Wendy knew was this."

   (Excerpt from *Peter Pan* by James M. Barrie)

3. "Today we depend for life's necessities almost wholly upon the activities of others. The work of thousands of human hands and thousands of human brains lies back of every meal you eat, every journey you take, every book you read, every bed in which you sleep, every telephone conversation, every telegram you receive, every garment you wear."

   (Excerpt from *How to Analyze People on Sight through the Science of Human Analysis: The Five Human Types* by Elsie Lincoln Benedict and Ralph Paine Benedict)

CHAPTER TAKEAWAYS

- A script needs to be easy on the ear and comfortable to the tongue.
- Smooth out a script by reading it out loud in its entirety and editing out anything that sounds funny or is difficult to say.
- Add phonetics to take the guesswork out of any challenging pronunciation.
- Mark words that you want to emphasize to bring out the meaning of each sentence.
- Follow the name stress principle, which calls for emphasis on the last word of a multiword name—Karin **Reed**.
- Place pauses, both short and power pauses.
- Beware of marking pitfalls:
  - Use a pencil on hard copy. Pen is usually impossible to erase.

- ▪ Misplaced emphasis can change the connotation.
- ▪ Make sure your implied contrast makes sense.
- ▪ Err on the side of fewer markings to avoid sounding stilted or unnatural.
- ▪ Emphasis and pauses are largely dependent on personal performance style. There may be several "right" answers.
- ▪ Listen to yourself to determine what sounds most natural.

SCRIPT MARKING EXERCISES ANSWER KEY

There are multiple acceptable answers for where to place pauses and what to emphasize for meaning. You will see what sounds right to my ears, but you may feel otherwise. Just be sure your version stresses the words that carry the meaning.

I opted for bold and slashes as my visual cues, but feel free to use whichever cue style suits you best.

1. "Either the well was very deep or she fell very slowly, for she had plenty of time as she went down to look about her and to wonder what was going to happen next." (Excerpt from *Alice's Adventures in Wonderland* by Lewis Carroll)

   My suggestion:
   *Either the **well** was very **deep** / or she **fell** very **slowly**, / for she had **plenty** of **time** as she went down / to **look about** her / and to **wonder** / what was going to happen **next**.*

   The caveman translation: "Well deep. Fell slowly. Plenty time look about wonder next." The essence of the passage is intact.

   I allowed myself to emphasize both *look* and *about* because the two words are so closely aligned. There are one-word synonyms that could easily take their place.

   You could also substitute a power pause for the short pause after *wonder* to build suspense if your style allows it.

2. "All children, except one, grow up. They soon know that they will grow up, and the way Wendy knew was this." (Excerpt from *Peter Pan* by James M. Barrie)

My suggestion:

*All children, / except **one**, // grow **up**. / They soon **know** that they will grow up, / and the way **Wendy** knew / was **this**. //*

You see that I placed two power pauses in this sentence. The first is designed to let that miraculous assertion sink in. The second is to create anticipation for what was to come. The author was going to reveal how Wendy found out about growing up.

Wendy is emphasized not only because she is a new character but also because it helps to draw out the contrast between Wendy and all children.

I didn't stress *grow* or *up* the second time because it was already introduced in the first sentence.

3. "Today we depend for life's necessities almost wholly upon the activities of others. The work of thousands of human hands and thousands of human brains lies back of every meal you eat, every journey you take, every book you read, every bed in which you sleep, every telephone conversation, every telegram you receive, every garment you wear." (Excerpt from *How to Analyze People on Sight through the Science of Human Analysis: The Five Human Types* by Elsie Lincoln Benedict and Ralph Paine Benedict.)

My suggestion:

*Today we **depend** for life's **necessities** / almost **wholly** upon the activities of **others**. / The work of **thousands** of human **hands** and thousands of human **brains** / lies back of every **meal** you eat, / every **journey** you take, / every **book** you read, / every **bed** in which you sleep, / every **telephone** conversation, / every **telegram** you receive, / every **garment** you wear.*

This passage is not ideal for reading aloud, but it is worth tackling because of the list. The parallel elements provide ample opportunity to draw the audience's ears to the most important words.

The first sentence is short, so I opted to only emphasize four words. I toyed with the idea of stressing "activities" as well, but it just sounded off.

The word *thousands* adds breadth to the concept of "others," while *hands* and *brains* provide specificity.

I stressed *every* only the first time I said it. Do you know why? Every other *every* would be old news and, therefore, not worthy of emphasis.

For the sake of parallelism, I emphasized each word that followed *every* because they carry the most meaning in the phrase with the exception of telephone. However, when I tried to emphasize *conversation* instead, it sounded odd to my ears. *Telephone conversation* follows the principle that if the last word in multiword entity is generic, you emphasize the second-to-last word. *Conversation* is the generic word. *Telephone* is the meaning word.

I only used short pauses rather than power pauses because I didn't feel one was justified per my own performance style.

NOTES

1. Nedra Lamar Newkirk and the Institute of Analytical Reading, *Giving the Sense: How to Read Aloud with Meaning.* Consultants Clearing House, Normandy Park, WA, 2016. Includes material from *How to Speak the Written Word: A Guide to Effective Public Reading.* Old Tappan, NJ: Fleming H. Revell, 1949.

2. Ibid.

CHAPTER 11

Tackling the Teleprompter

oe to the person who underestimates the challenges of reading off a teleprompter. After all, how hard can it be? It's just *reading*.

Teleprompters can give a false sense of security. The words are all there, so the assumption is that you don't have to think. Just ask Michael Bay.

BLOCKBUSTER DIRECTOR BOMBS ON STAGE

The Consumer Electronics Show (CES) is one of the biggest conventions held annually in Las Vegas. The event in 2014 was no different. Companies pull out all the stops and bring in major star power to attract attention to their latest offerings.

Samsung was introducing its curved television that year and thought "who better than Michael Bay, director of blockbusters like the *Transformers* movies, to enthusiastically endorse the 'revolutionary technology'?" He was booked to appear on the CES stage as a celebrity spokesperson of a sort.

Joe Stinziano, Samsung's executive vice president, served as emcee and invited Bay to join him in front of the audience of hundreds of journalists and industry insiders. Bay began his performance just fine. He asked how everyone was doing and then said, "My job as a director is I get to dream for a living."

Stinziano then asked him how he comes up with the larger-than-life ideas in his movies. At this point, Bay starts answering the question while looking at the teleprompter. He then looks away, then back at the prompter, before saying, "The type is all off. I'm sorry, but I'll just wing this."

Stinziano tries to keep him on track by lobbing some softball questions at him, to no avail. Then, a moment forever trapped in social media history: Stinziano asks, "The curve . . . how do you think it's going to impact how people experience your movies?"

Bay responds with a terse, "Excuse me. I'm sorry. I'm sorry" before walking off stage, never to return.

You cannot watch the video without feeling terrible for the guy's cringe-worthy appearance.

Michael Bay is undoubtedly a smart guy, and he has said that he's gone on stage "a couple hundred times" without incident and spoken intelligently. So what happened?

According to Bay, he had accidentally "jumped a line," and the prompter operator started scrolling the text up and down, in a desperate attempt to find the proper place in the copy.

The director of *Transformers* was transformed into the butt of late-night jokes.

LESSONS LEARNED FROM MICHAEL BAY'S IMPLOSION

Michael Bay was interviewed the next day by *TMZ Live*, a celebrity news web site, and he offered a postmortem of what went wrong. His explanation of what he called "a human moment" provides insightful instruction on how to avoid a full-fledged flame-out when using a teleprompter.[1]

Lesson 1: Know Your Content

Bay told *TMZ* that he had arrived the night before his performance and gone straight to bed. The show was the following morning. He made no mention of rehearsing but did point out that he was going to be talking about some "very technical jargon."

Although Bay has impressive directing and producing chops, this topic was out of his realm of expertise, which made him less confident in his ability to "wing it." He said he could see the audience was "serious about its electronic products," and he was "afraid he was going to embarrass himself more."

Without a deep base of domain knowledge from which to pull, Bay was vulnerable. When the technical rug was pulled out from under him, he felt like he was left with no choice. He opted for exiting rather than sounding stupid.

Just because the words will presumably be there for you doesn't mean you don't need to know what you're talking about. There's no guarantee that your script will be there, no matter how many reassurances you are given in advance. Technology is not fail-safe, and human error is real. It is not mandatory for you to memorize your script, but you should be comfortable enough with the content that you can hit the major points if the prompter goes out.

You need to protect yourself. After all, even if it was the teleprompter operator's fault, no one was laughing at the prompter operator the next day. They were laughing at Michael Bay.

Lesson 2: Know Your Script

In the *TMZ* interview, Michael Bay laments the fact that "they kept rewriting the script, rewriting the script." Even if he had practiced in advance, any time spent on smoothing out the delivery would have been for naught if the script he was going to perform was different.

It is tempting to want to edit copy over and over again, but there are diminishing returns. A brilliantly worded script delivered sloppily is worthless. Make sure you give yourself enough time to practice the script you will be performing. If you are not writing it, put your foot down on last-minute edits. Explain that your performance will suffer if you don't have time to practice, and that won't be good for anyone.

Lesson 3: Stay in the Moment

The most perplexing aspect of Michael Bay's bombing was his inability to answer some pretty simple questions: How do you come up with the ideas for your movies? How will the curve change how people experience your movies?

If he were asked those questions today, he surely could come up with answers that are at least coherent. But Bay told his *TMZ* interviewers that he would not have been able to answer even a basic question about his career. He wouldn't have heard the question, because there was another booming voice, the one inside his head, saying, "We gotta fix this glitch." His inner critic had hijacked his performance and rendered him helpless.

As tough as it is when you know you've made a mistake, obsessing about what happened in the past only amplifies the problem. If you devote too much of your energy on what has already happened, your subsequent performance suffers. Force yourself to stay in the moment, so you don't derail the rest of your presentation.

The major takeaway from Michael Bay's epic fail is this: a teleprompter is not an autopilot for your brain. While it is a useful tool, it still requires mental preparation and focus during the performance. Without those two elements, you run the risk of becoming fodder for a blooper reel.

TELEPROMPTER-FRIENDLY COPY: BEST PRACTICES

Software applications for teleprompter come on the market on a regular basis, and the lack of universality can create problems when it comes to transferring your document to prompter text.

The way your script appears in your document may be very different from how it appears once it is loaded into the prompter. The software may not like your version of Word and inserts its own characters—or even worse, it makes them disappear.

Read Your Script in the Prompter *before* Your Performance

When I serve as a moderator of webcasts, I am often scripted at the end to direct viewers to a web site for more information. The address is usually a bit tricky, but I take my time saying it to make sure my audience can jot it down. Sometimes, though, that web site address never makes it to the prompter, which comes as a surprise to everyone, including me. The line starts out fine and says, "For more information, please go to . . ." but instead of saying something like "www-dot [blah, blah, blah]," there's just a big blank space where the address *should* have been. This could easily turn into a blooper reel moment, but thankfully, I can easily read the address off my hard copy, which I always keep on set with me in the event something like this happens.

The culprit was a clunky translation between the document software and the teleprompter software. When the script was imported into the prompter, it could not make sense of the hyperlink the Web address defaulted to in the Microsoft Word document. Consequently, it just left the address out.

This is just one argument for checking out your script in the prompter prior to your performance. Sometimes, the prompter software speaks the same language as the document, but if it doesn't, you want to find out ahead of time.

Long numbers and words can also create awkward spacing on the screen. Depending on font size, the number of characters per line can be severely limiting. If you have several multisyllabic words in a row, you could end up with each word taking up a whole line and look like this:

The capital is a

cosmopolitan,

idiosyncratic,

commercializat

ion hotbed.

Not the most reader-friendly text. At a minimum, you need to be aware of the potential pitfall. At most, you may want to change it.

The same holds true for numbers. If you are in the seven figures or more, make sure the numerals don't wrap around to look something like this:

7,000,000,0

00

You would be better off writing it as "7 million" anyway. You avoid the possibility of the numerals not fitting properly. Plus, zeros can be difficult to process on the fly in the prompter.

Effective Visual Cues in Teleprompter Copy

Analyzing your script for emphasis and phrasing does not have to end with the printed page. The marks can be added to the teleprompter copy as well and can serve as visual cues throughout your performance.

There are several options for both stress and pauses. Choose the one that works best for you. This might require some experimentation along the way. Perhaps you will create your own marks that do the trick. Just be sure they help rather than hinder your performance.

Options for Marking Emphasis

The most important consideration for selecting how you are going to indicate emphasis is to choose one that will be immediately recognizable to you. You want your visual cue to produce an automatic response, not require additional processing.

Here are some common options for marking emphasis:

- **Bold**

  When initially discussing how to mark copy for stress, I used **bold** to indicate the words to emphasize. If this works for you, by all means use it. However, this option does have some limitations. Sometimes all of the words are put in bold to make them stand out on the screen. Ask the prompter operator before choosing this option.

- ALL CAPS

    Using all caps takes the guesswork out of it. I have never seen it become lost in translation when loaded into prompter software. The only danger is how you may react to all caps. Sometimes, it can cause speakers to overemphasize or shout the words. Try it out and be ready to choose another option if you hear yourself go beyond natural stress. (If you are hoarse after your performance, that's another sign you need to try something different.)

- Underline

    Underlining is the most similar option to how you likely mark your hard copy. If you have practiced reading off the printed page with stressed words underlined, then this might feel most comfortable to you.

    A word of warning: not all prompter software reads underlines. At one of my training sites, participants sent over their scripts to the prompter software after meticulously marking them with underlining for stress. Unfortunately, as soon as the copy was loaded into the prompter, all of the underlining disappeared. The prompter operator manually inserted the underlines by cross referencing the original script, but it was laborious for the prompter operator and nerve-racking for the performers who were horrified to find their hard work was lost, if only temporarily.

To avoid uncertainty, ask the teleprompter operator in advance what file format works best with the prompter software. Sometimes, it's just a matter of saving the script in a different version, as a .doc rather than a .docx, which is a simple fix.

Options for Marking Pauses

As with marking for emphasis, how you identify places to pause also comes down to personal preference. Here are some common options for marking your pauses:

- Slashes

    The slashes reflect what is most commonly used on the printed page and therefore may be the best bet for you. You can indicate a short pause with a / and a power pause with //.

    I did have a student balk at the use of the slashes, though, because her brain wanted to process them as letters rather than visual cues to pause. She opted for a mark that she could not mistake for a letter *L*.

■ Ellipses

Ellipses have the advantage of inserting physical space into a sentence, which also makes it an effective trigger for the speaker to physically pause. The eyes have to bounce through the . . . before moving onto the next phrase. Ellipses can also be picked up by peripheral vision and can provide advanced warning of an upcoming stop in the action.

There is no way to distinguish a short pause from a power pause with this option, though.

■ Hyphens

A hyphen or dash can be a useful reminder to pause appropriately. One dash (—) can be used to indicate a short pause. Two dashes (— —) can indicated a power pause.

The only drawback of this option is how common hyphens are in our syntax. A hyphenated word may be mistaken for a place to pause. Proceed with caution.

■ Extra space created by the Return key

I consider this the "nuclear option." For those workshop participants who just can't help themselves and refuse to pause, I force them into periodic silence by inserting extra space in the prompter via the Return key. Remember, there are only so many lines visible at one time on the screen. The on-camera performer can't forge ahead through the copy if he or she has to wait for it to scroll up. It ends up looking something like this:

How much wood would
a woodchuck chuck

if a woodchuck could
chuck wood?

There is no hard-and-fast rule saying you can't use a combination of options to indicate both stress and phrasing. For example, if you want to use ellipses but need a visual cue for a power pause, you can use ellipses (. . .) for the short pauses and the Return key to add extra space in your prompter script as a reminder of a power pause.

Visual Cues Are Guides, Not Absolutes

A cue, by definition, is "a hint; intimation; guiding suggestion." And the visual cues indicating emphasis and phrasing are just that: guiding suggestions—they are not absolutes.

The worst thing you could take away from this exercise is to become hyperfocused on obeying the cues and forget about the meaning behind the words you are saying. Remember, marking for stress and pauses is a way to recapture natural speech patterns often lost when reading. If you concentrate more on *what* you are saying than *how* you are saying it, most of you will automatically stress the appropriate words and pause at the spots that make sense.

Visual cues are just a tool that you have in your toolbox—it is up to you whether you want to pull them out or keep them tucked away. If you find that the markings in the teleprompter script are distracting, use them sparingly or take them away completely. I definitely use fewer visual cues today than I did at the start of my career, but for challenging scripts, they are still a lifesaver for me.

THE ROLE OF THE TELEPROMPTER OPERATOR

When I began my career in TV news, I did not have the luxury of a teleprompter operator. I controlled my own prompter by foot pedal, which required multitasking of the "pat your belly and scratch your head at the same time" order.

Back then, the scripts were printed out, taped together, and put on a conveyor belt of a sort. The pages then somehow magically appeared in the prompter in front of me . . . or didn't.

When I sat down at the desk to anchor my very first newscast in 1992, I was confident I had everything in place. The scripts were written, the video was ready to roll, and I had composed the perfect anchor helmet (aka hairdo). The opening credits ran, and I put my foot on the pedal, ready to engage.

The red light on the camera lit up on cue, and I introduced myself and read the first sentence. I pressed the prompter pedal to move to the next paragraph, but instead of the words scrolling up, they scrolled down and then completely off the screen.

The prompter pedal also had a dial on the side, which I had ignored. Unfortunately, that dial dictated whether the conveyor belt went forward or in reverse. You can guess where that dial was stuck.

I managed to use my stack of scripts in front of me to make it to the next commercial break. Even to this day, I laugh when I see anchors sitting at their desks without any hard copy. Don't they know they are walking a tightrope without a net?

Having spent so many years without one, I have utmost appreciation for the teleprompter operator. After all, he or she can play a pivotal role in your on-camera success.

Let me explain what the prompter operator can and cannot do.

A Second Set of Eyes

The teleprompter operator is the first person who sees the script once it is loaded into the prompter software. Typically, he or she will go through the script and catch any typos, misspellings, or grammatical errors before you even have a chance to check it out.

Prompter operators are looking out for you. I have been saved from embarrassment many, many times by prompter operators who have seen problems in the script before I did.

Adjusting Font Size

The prompter operator is not only a second set of eyes but can also adjust the font to help *your* eyes see the text clearly. There should be no need to squint—if the words are too small for you to read them comfortably, just ask the operator if he or she can make the font size bigger.

Remember, the prompter operator is there to help you perform at your best. If you are struggling to see the copy, that's an easy fix.

Following the Leader

One of the more common complaints I hear after students have logged their first performance using a teleprompter is: "The prompter guy kept speeding up." This could not be further from the truth.

Remember, the teleprompter operator is following *you*, you are not following the teleprompter operator. If you feel like the words are scrolling faster, in all likelihood, it is merely reflecting your own increasing pace. It is not uncommon for on-camera performers who have never used a teleprompter to be tempted to read faster to ensure the words come out of their mouths before they are sucked off the screen.

A good prompter operator will go right at your pace and will adjust it accordingly. If you use a power pause, the words on the prompter will stay put until you pick back up again.

Trust that the teleprompter operator has your back. You have enough to worry about—take disappearing text off your list.

Editing on the Fly

The fact that the copy is loaded into the prompter does not mean it is set in stone. The prompter operator is able and willing to edit on the fly.

Say you keep tripping up on a certain word and want to change it. The prompter operator has the flexibility at any time to edit it to your specifications. Sometimes, you don't even have to ask.

During a live broadcast, I was interviewing a panelist whose first name was Bernd. For some reason, I had not written down the phonetics in my script and mispronounced it. I called him "BURNT" but I should have called him "BEARNT." After I botched it, my eagle-eyed (and -eared) prompter operator went through the script and changed every mention of his name to the phonetic spelling of "BEARNT." I pronounced it correctly for the rest of the show. (Thank you, Gary.)

No Mind Reading

One of the most difficult on-camera maneuvers to perform is combining scripted text with ad-libbing—especially unplanned ad-libbing.

It is challenging for you because it can be very difficult to go off prompter, say something coherently, and then smoothly transition back to the text on the screen.

It is also tough for the teleprompter operator whose primary purpose is to follow you. But if you wander off script, the prompter operator can't go with you. Sometimes, that causes them to panic.

They might scroll abruptly up and down to try to find the right place in the script. (Remember Michael Bay?) Imagine ad-libbing while watching words flying erratically in front of your face.

If you do think you will go off script, at least warn the prompter operator that you plan to do so. That will eliminate the unnecessary and heart-pounding search for the proper prompter spot. You may even want to add a note in the copy saying "[AD-LIB]" where you think you might start to riff. The prompter operator will know to keep the text on the screen until you return to it.

Adjusting the Read Line

Did you know there is a visual guide on the prompter screen, which tells you what line you should be reading at any given time?

It can take different forms, but the most common one is in the shape of a small triangle on the left side of the screen, sometimes referred to as the read line guide. (Read rhymes with heed.) The prompter operator attempts to match whatever line that triangle is pointing to, to the words that are coming out of your mouth.

Typically, the read line guide is located about a third of the way down from the top of the screen. It is high enough to allow the speaker to detect upcoming pauses or emphasis words in his or her peripheral vision, but it's also low enough to provide a bit of cushion. As discussed earlier, the greatest fear people have when using a prompter is that the words will roll away. With the read line guide a third of the way down, the words you just said should still be on the screen just in case.

That being said, if you want to change the location of the read line, the prompter operator can change it. If you want to have it halfway down instead of a third, that triangle can be moved to fit your needs.

I would not recommend having the read line guide at the bottom of the screen unless you are an adrenaline junkie and love the element of surprise.

PROMPTER PRACTICE MADE POSSIBLE

Not too long ago, teleprompters were reserved for formal video productions or high-end live events. Companies that didn't have their own production folks in house would hire outside firms to provide prompting services, complete with top-notch equipment, software, and prompter professionals who would run it.

If a company or production house goes to the trouble of hiring a teleprompter firm, it is likely a high-stakes situation. So imagine if you walk into this shoot, ready to go on-camera. You have never even seen a teleprompter, let alone read off of one, and your first time doing so will be in what is already a high-pressure environment.

A little practice reading off of a prompter in advance would have been nice, but the technology is simply not accessible. Or is it?

The Proliferation of Prompter Software

Teleprompting has spread to the masses thanks to prompter software readily available on laptops, tablets, and smartphones. In fact, many smaller production houses and companies with limited production budgets have invested in equipment, which turns tablets into viable teleprompter rigs. What this means for you is that you finally have a way to practice reading off a prompter before it really counts.

Prompter apps are available for Windows and OS X, and usually come in both professional and novice versions. They vary in terms of how scripts are loaded or imported into the application, but they all can convert documents into scrolling text.

Because these apps are often used with a teleprompter rig that has reflective glass, the text can be put into mirror mode, which allows the words to appear properly on the prompter. However, for practice purposes, you can simply use full-screen mode unless you have decided you really, really need the full setup.

Control the Scroll

My first prompter software did not allow you to control the speed of the scrolling. Instead, you chose one speed, and you were stuck with it from beginning to end. Now you have many options. If you are using a laptop, scrolling can typically be controlled by the arrow keys, mouse, or track pad. Some apps allow you to vary the speed using another device connected via Bluetooth. Many prompter software companies sell accessories like foot pedals and handheld remote controls. The key is to make sure the accessories are compatible with the device running the prompter software.

If you are leery of trying to control the scrolling speed while reading off the prompter, look for prompter software with voice recognition. The lines move as your device hears you say them. You can even go completely off-script, and the words will stay put until you return to the text on the screen. Truly amazing. However, if the room is noisy or the device picking up your voice is too far away, the accuracy of the scrolling may be compromised. You may need to invest in an external microphone that is designed to work with your laptop, phone, or tablet.

Watch Yourself

Another consideration is whether you'd like to record yourself while using the teleprompter app. Some software uses the front-facing camera on your device to record your performance. Your image is projected on the screen so you can actually adjust how you are framing yourself before starting to record. Once the words start scrolling, the text will be in the foreground but your image will be in the background to ensure you don't move out of frame. This is a great way to assess your performance, but seeing yourself in the background might distract you.

LOST IN THE TELEPROMPTER

No matter how much you practice or how proficient your teleprompter operator may be, you still may get lost in the prompter. Maybe you looked away temporarily and couldn't find your place when you looked back. Or maybe you skipped a line by accident. It happens, but how you handle it makes a difference.

Some speakers try to keep talking, hoping they will babble their way back to the topic at hand, but this option can easily lead to blunders. It gets back to that key piece of advice from my colleague: "Don't start talking unless you have something to say." When you lose yourself in the prompter, don't keep talking unless you have something to say.

A better option is to pause and take a look at the words on the screen. Try to ascertain what concept you were trying to relay, and attempt to bring your sentence to a quick close and then bridge to the next sentence as smoothly as possible. The pause to regroup and find your way back is a much better option than talking continuously in circles.

CHAPTER TAKEAWAYS

- A teleprompter is not autopilot for your brain.
- Know your content and your script just in case the prompter fails.
- Read your script in the teleprompter before your performance to avoid any surprises in formatting.
- Use visual cues indicating emphasis and pauses to guide you through your performance.
- The prompter operator is following you. You are not following the prompter operator.
- If you plan to ad lib, mark it in the script and warn your prompter operator.
- If you get lost in the teleprompter, do not babble. Collect your thoughts and bridge to the next topic or sentence.

NOTE

1. You can watch Michael Bay's *TMZ Live* interview at https://www.youtube.com/watch?v=zdEcRNSrJD4.

SECTION
SIX

The Most Common On-Camera Performance Scenarios

Today, we communicate through cameras all the time in both our personal and professional lives. The expectation that we can watch overwhelms our willingness to read or even just listen. Those who are camera-phobic can lament this cultural change or embrace it and learn to leverage it.

Not all on-camera performance scenarios are created equal. Some are easier to navigate than others and each comes with its own challenges. In this section, I take a deep dive into some specific on-camera scenarios that you are likely to encounter. The section is divided into the following chapters:

- Chapter 12: Presenting Directly to the Camera in a Studio Setting
- Chapter 13: Videoconferencing and Interviews via Video Chat
- Chapter 14: Webcasts—Best Practices for Panelists and Moderators
- Chapter 15: Broadcast Interview Basics

Presenting Directly to the Camera in a Studio Setting

Here's the situation: You've been approached by someone in your communications department to appear on camera. Maybe it's for the company web site. Maybe it's for a marketing video for a product launch. Maybe it's an employee profile for the corporate YouTube channel.

Your first reaction is that you're flattered to be asked. But perhaps the more overwhelming second reaction is this: you're pretty nervous about it—possibly even terrified. Or perhaps you are on the other side of the spectrum and embrace the opportunity to engage in the exploding media landscape. After all, it offers unprecedented opportunity for you to get your message out there.

Regardless of your gut-level response, appearing on-camera is no longer reserved for communication professionals, actors, and any other brand of what is called "on-camera talent." No matter where you are on the corporate food chain, you may be asked at some point to serve as a de facto spokesperson.

I began my training in response to this shift. I developed my curriculum with the goal of demystifying communicating through the camera with the MVPs of Performance Success as the centerpiece.

This chapter will help you solidify the techniques covered so far by walking you through the corporate video process from a talent perspective, breaking it down into four main segments:

- Preparing for the Shoot
- Orienting Yourself to the Studio
- Performing at Your Best
- Reviewing Your Performance

▶ **NOTE**

Here's a quick vocabulary lesson for those who are new to "the biz": "talent" means the person appearing on camera, and "shoot" means when the video is shot.

I will reinforce some of what you've already learned and offer some new concepts in a lifelike framework. But first, I'll give you a bit of perspective, in a broad sense, on how best to use video across the corporate landscape.

CONSIDERATIONS FOR CORPORATE VIDEO

Video is not intended to serve as a visual version of a white paper. Video as a medium is best for eliciting emotion and inspiring a viewer to go elsewhere to find out more. It is not the proper vehicle for relaying vast amounts of information.

When people read the written word, they have the luxury of going back and rereading parts that perhaps confused them the first time through or were of greater interest. They can take notes or highlight key takeaways, processing the information a second time by either putting it into their own words or visually culling out the critical words.

When someone watches a video, they will perhaps pick up a fact or two, but video as a means of transferring dense information falls short. However, that doesn't mean it isn't powerful.

A Lesson from TV News

As a TV news reporter, I was often given an assignment on a broad topic but forced to boil it down to fit into a 90-second slot on the nightly news. This held true no matter how complex or multifaceted the subject matter was. My favorite approach to this challenge was to take that expansive topic and make it real by focusing on one person who illustrated the issue at hand.

Let's say I was asked to do a story about the homeless problem in the area. I could have put together a piece laden with graphics, citing statistics and sources. It would be fact-filled and informative . . . and utterly forgettable.

Recognizing these limitations, I would opt for a different approach. Instead, I would choose to profile a single mother living out of her car with her two young children because she couldn't find affordable housing. She would speak of her journey with raw emotion that was nowhere to be found in the numbers tallied by social service agencies.

That second approach made people care. It would prompt viewers to call the station to find out what they could do to help. Any time our audience was shown a story about a person truly in need, they responded with unimaginable compassion in tangible ways. Sometimes it translated into donations of thousands of fans for those who didn't have air conditioning during a heat wave. Sometimes it meant mounds of donated winter coats, ready to be given out to those who would've suffered through the winter chill.

Humanizing a story inspires action; numbers do not. The power of video is in the emotions it can stir.

A common mistake made when creating corporate video is trying to convey too much information. This results in either a video that is way too long or a shorter one that is way too dense.

Consider what you are hoping to inspire your viewer to do, and then use your video to inspire them to take that action.

Does Length Matter?

A corporate video may not have the same strict time parameters as a story produced to wedge into a network newscast. However, understanding audience attention span is vital.

How long should a video be? There are a plethora of answers to that question, but allow me to offer some insight from Wistia, one of the largest online video hosting platforms. In 2016, Wistia analyzed how much of a video a viewer would watch relative to the total length of the video, and they had an enormous data set to analyze for the research: 564,710 videos and more than 1.3 billion plays. What they found was the shorter the video, the more of it the viewer was willing to consume, as shown in Figure 12.1.

The sweet spot for video length appears to be two minutes, according to this research with a significant drop off in viewership between two and six minutes. That being said, while erring on the side of brevity is a good choice, a video that is compelling and crafted beautifully will likely still keep its audience engaged even if it's a little on the longer side.

However, this should not keep you from front-loading your key takeaways. All videos in the study showed a drop in viewership, even those less than one minute long.

If you are organizing for the ear, make sure they hear the core message, loud and clear, early on.

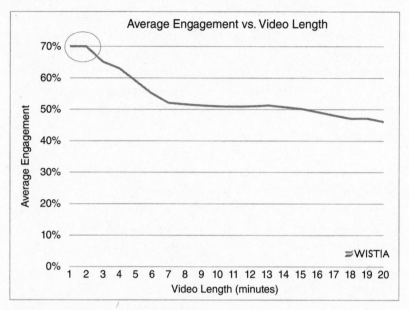

Figure 12.1 Wistia Video Analytics Graph
Source: Ezra Fishman, Wistia.com, "How Long Should Your Next Video Be?," July 5, 2016, https://wistia.com/blog/optimal-video-length

How Much Face Time Is *Too* Much?

A stellar-quality video may earn its extra length, but beware the dangers of extending your own face time on camera without interruption. You can easily overstay your welcome.

If you are speaking directly to the camera without any graphics or video interwoven, do not attempt to speak beyond two minutes. TV time can be measured in dog years. Even one minute can feel like seven, and our attention spans are shortening.

Remember, we are wired to seek out change in our environment. If your viewer's only option is to stare at your mug for any longer than two minutes, you run the risk of them turning you off or tuning you out. That holds true for even the most animated among us.

Plus, think about the focus required to pull off a great performance. The longer you are on camera without a break, the harder it will be to sustain the high level of concentration and energy it requires.

If you feel like you have too much to say and two minutes is simply not enough time, think of a way to break it up. Instead of recording one long video, create several shorter ones. You will likely give a better presentation during those brief bursts, and your viewer will have more control over how he or she consumes your content.

PREPARING FOR THE SHOOT

What happens before the video is actually shot largely depends on whether or not you are in control of the content.

For this exercise, we will assume that you have creative control, meaning you have ultimate say over what you will say. We will also assume that you will be reading a script off prompter.

Creating Your Content

If there is one thing I would want you to remember above all else when it comes to creating content, it is this: organize according to the Rule of Three. That also would be my core message for this particular section and would head up my framework I introduced to you in Chapter 8, "Organizing for the Ear."

Once you have established your core message, choose your three supporting points. Not two, not four—and definitely not five or six. Too much information means no staying power.

Here's what my Rule of Three framework would look like:

1. Humans process information in patterns.
2. Three is the smallest number to create a pattern.
3. Brevity + Pattern = Memorable Content.

If time allows, you can expand the Rule of Three into subpoints, but keep in mind how quickly time flies on camera. A two-minute script is often only one page, double-spaced.

Identifying Your Viewer

What you want to say and how you want to say it is dictated by your viewer. The tone and level of detail must meet the needs of your audience.

If your topic is technical but you know your audience is very familiar with the terms and concepts, you can get away with speaking at a higher level of detail than if you were speaking to an audience without domain knowledge.

Your tone also depends on your relationship with the viewer. As you learned earlier, a conversation through a camera is an intimate one, much like talking across the dinner table. But your dinner guest might be a neighbor or your manager—and you probably wouldn't talk to them the same way.

Once you determine who your viewer is and how that will impact your approach, you are ready to write.

Writing the Way You Speak

If you write your entire script without ever saying the words aloud, you will likely encounter some unexpected challenges once you do try to perform it on camera. Remember, the way the words sound in your head is never the way they sound coming out of your mouth.

A dictation app can take all the guesswork out of writing the way you speak because you are actually speaking your script, minus the typing. If that is too extreme, at least give voice to the words periodically to make sure they flow well. Your delivery should not require verbal gymnastics. Think in terms of short, action-oriented sentences. And keep an eye out for power pause opportunities for the sake of variety and impact.

Once your script is complete, read it out loud in its entirety. The script should be easy on the ear and comfortable to the tongue. Ask for guidance on the former from colleagues. Easy on the ear means the message is easily understood. Rely on your gut for the latter. Comfortable to the tongue means you can deliver it smoothly without getting tripped up.

When in doubt, edit it out.

Marking for Meaning

Once the script is solid and phonetics have been added where necessary, you can go through the meticulous process of marking for meaning.

Select the words to stress based on how much meaning they carry in the sentence. Do they represent new ideas for the viewer? If you did not stress them, would some of the critical essence of the sentence be lost? Try it out in caveman-speak and see if the gist of the sentence is still intact.

Mark your script using the visual cue of choice, but make sure it will comply with the teleprompter software. You don't want to show up to perform your script and find that all of the markings were wiped out when it was loaded into the prompter. As you learned in the previous chapter, the basic emphasis options for prompter are **bold**, ALL CAPS, and underline.

The next step involves placing pauses. A short pause separates ideas and concepts. A power pause gives space for the audience to contemplate what was just said or creates anticipation for what will be said next. The basic options to indicate pauses are slashes, hyphens, ellipses, or physical space created by the Return key. The markings can also be used in combination.

Practice, Practice, Practice

You may be someone who thrives on spontaneity, but unless you are an absolute on-camera pro, do not try to wing it. While you will not have access to the studio prior to the record, you can still practice performing your script, and you can go as low-tech or high-tech as you want.

- **Low-tech.** Simply practice reading your script off the printed page. Once you get the flow of the words down, you will have one less thing to worry about when you perform it in the studio.
- **Low-tech but a bit more realistic.** Print the script in a large font and tape it to a mirror or wall. You will be able to work not only on how you deliver it vocally but also on your body language. If you know how you will be framed, think about how that will affect your gestures. Remember, the wider the shot, the more freedom you have to move.
- **High-tech.** Use a prompter app on your laptop, phone, or tablet to practice reading your script off a teleprompter. The interface

may not be exactly like the one you will use in the studio, but it will provide a useful approximation. It will also allow you to play with actually looking away from the lens periodically as you would in normal conversation.

- **High-tech with playback.** Record yourself using your prompter app and then play back your performance. Often, you have to see with your own eyes what you are doing wrong in order to correct it. Better to catch potential issues while practicing than to find out while on set for the real thing.

Looking the Part

Your on-camera wardrobe must be in line with the expectations of your audience. If your viewer will most likely be wearing a coat and tie, then you had better, too. Conversely, someone sporting a T-shirt and flip-flops might consider you out of touch if you are delivering your message to him while donning a Brooks Brothers three-piece suit.

Once you know what section of your closet you should go to, think about what colors and styles will play well on camera. You can use Table 12.1 as a cheat sheet.

Microphone Matters

If you know in advance that you will be using a wireless lavaliere microphone, think about where the microphone itself can be clipped onto your clothes as well as where the battery pack/transmitter can sit out of sight.

Table 12.1 What to Wear and What *Not* to Wear on Camera

What to Wear	What Not to Wear
Solids	Small patterns (checks, tweeds, or stripes)
Colors that compliment your complexion	All black, all white, or overly vibrant red
Tailored pieces with clean lines	Bulky, unstructured layers that might add weight
Makeup to reduce shine (men and women) Additional makeup to define eyes and lips (women)	Jewelry, including watches, that might interfere with audio or distract the viewer

The battery pack/transmitter is about the size of a pack of cigarettes and can either hang from a belt or waistband or be put in a pocket, provided the pants are baggy enough that there won't be an unsightly bulge.

The microphone, while not heavy, requires something sturdy enough to handle its weight. Lightweight fabrics like silk or rayon have a tendency to fold where the microphone is clipped. The microphone may then rub against the fabric and create extra audio feedback that can't be edited out.

V-neck shirts, blouses, or dresses provide ideal landing spots for microphones, allowing them to be positioned evenly under the chin. Jewel-neck or round-neck tops that come close to the collarbone can pose problems because the microphone gets buried in the hollow of the neck, muffling the sound.

Hair Issues

Your long lustrous locks might be the envy of many, but on camera, they may be your enemy. Hair falling into your eyes can be distracting for your viewer, as can repeated attempts to sweep it away from your face in mid performance. If you choose to keep part of your hair falling in front of your shoulder, you run the risk of having it swish against the microphone. A perfect take could be ruined by troublesome tresses. The safest avenue is to pull it back if you think your style might pose problems.

Bangs can also cast unwanted shadows if the lighting can't accommodate for them. Even if you have never worn hairspray in your life, invest in a can just for on-camera performances. Keeping bangs away from your face is a must.

Getting Rid of Your Fifth Appendage

Yes, our smartphones have become a part of us, and the idea of leaving them behind may seem cruel. However, a buzzing, beeping, ringing, or singing smartphone has no place in a studio. And I assume you're not planning to answer your phone in the middle of your performance.

Our phones are always distractions of the highest degree, and you do not need any more while you are managing your way through your on-camera moment. Plus, cell phones can cause interference in the audio. It doesn't happen all the time, but if it happens during your favorite take, one time is all that matters.

ORIENTING YOURSELF TO THE STUDIO

You have crafted a memorable message with your viewer in mind. You have perfected and marked your script, and it is now in the hands of the teleprompter operator. You have picked out a camera-friendly outfit (or two) and are ready for your close-up, Mr. DeMille.

You show up at the studio and find a whole host of people there to greet you. Who *are* all of these people?

Meet the Crew

The size of the studio crew often depends on the budget and the scope of the project. Over the years, I have worked with a crew of 1 all the way up to a crew of 20.

Sometimes, you, the talent, won't even see some of the crew members, because they are in another room—especially if it's a live broadcast or live to tape, meaning the show will be taped as if it were live. On those occasions, the director sits in what is called the control room, often with the producer, which allows them to freely discuss what is happening or what is about to happen during the actual recording of the performance. They can't be in the studio because their voices would be picked up by the microphones.

In this section, I will describe the members of the production crew whom you most likely will meet face to face with the assumption that the producer and director are out of sight.

The Floor Director

The floor director is the person who serves as the air traffic controller of the studio crew. He or she is the one who receives instructions from the director or producer and then disseminates them to the rest of the crew.

The floor director is also the person who does what's called a *countdown* and then cues you to start talking. You will find him or her standing in close proximity to the camera into which you will be speaking.

When the floor director gets word that the rest of the crew is ready to either go live or record, he or she will count you down so everyone will be in sync. It will go something like this: "In 5-4-3-2-*[silent beat]*," and then he or she will give you a visual cue, letting you know that you can begin talking.

That visual cue is often a matter of personal style. Sometimes, a floor director will simply point at you or the camera. Periodically, a floor director will get creative and offer his or her own Sammy Sosa, peace-out sign. Regardless, the cue is rarely subtle, so don't worry about missing it.

You may be wondering why the floor director doesn't count all the way down to one. The microphone you are wearing is not always "live" but will most definitely be turned on right before you speak. If the floor director says "one," there's a chance his or her voice might be heard a split second before you say your first words or even as you are saying your first words if you jump your cue. You, the talent, are expected to silently count one in your head, and then speak when the floor director physically cues you to begin.

The Audio Technician

The audio technician gets up close and personal with you, mainly because he or she needs to put the microphone on you. Audio techs will be especially appreciative of your carefully selected wardrobe that gives them easy access to a spot for the transmitter pack to hang. A sheath dress is the stuff of nightmares.

The audio tech will also find the best place to clip your microphone, preferably a place where there's no chance of it rubbing against part of your clothing, hair, or jewelry.

There is no need to project your voice when wearing a microphone for on-camera work. Part of the audio technician's job is to set proper volume levels. He or she will adjust the volume based on the level at which you naturally speak. In order to do that, they will ask you to say a few words or even count down from 10. It's your intelligence test.

Quick note: If you need to take a bio break, you might want to let your audio technician know, so he or she can either disconnect the transmitter or at least turn the mic off. There's no need to broadcast your bodily functions.

The Camera Operator

In a studio setting, the cameras are typically handled by a camera operator who takes instruction on framing the shot from the director. He or she will make sure there is nothing in the frame that shouldn't be there (light stands, duct tape, odd reflections) and will sometimes adjust framing during a performance if the talent's movements require it.

If you are having trouble reading the teleprompter because the camera is too far away, ask the camera operator if it would be possible to move closer. Usually, that is not a problem.

Expect the camera to be at eye level the majority of the time. If you feel like you are looking down or up, ask if that is by design. This is especially common when there is a big disparity between the height of the talent and the height of the camera operator. Looking directly into the lens will offer the most flattering and natural angle.

If the performance requires multiple cameras, as in the case of a webcast, there will be several camera operators on set at one time.

Remember to ask how you are being framed so you can give some thought to how much room you have to move and gesture.

The Teleprompter Operator

In the previous chapter, you learned about the important role the teleprompter operator plays in your performance success. Sometimes, the prompter operator is in the studio, but sometimes, he or she is in the control room with the director and/or producer.

Regardless of where the prompter operator is during the performance, know you can always request his or her help with prompter edits. If the prompter operator is in the control room, the floor director can relay any information to him or her.

The Crew's Mission

What's important to remember about any and every member of the crew is they are there to help you be your best. Your goal should not be to get them out in record time (even though no one would complain if you knocked it out of the park on the first take.)

They want you to come away from the experience satisfied with how you did and pleased with the final product. It doesn't matter to the crew whether you do 2 takes or 20 takes. They are invested in your on-camera success, and they are more than willing to wait for it.

Give Yourself the Once-Over

Unless you have a designated makeup person, you are your final line of defense when it comes to your appearance. A member of the crew may notice the piece of spinach in your teeth, but they are also focusing on myriad other things and may miss it.

Always look in the mirror before you get in front of the camera and give yourself one last once-over. Do you have any hair sticking out? Do you indeed have food in your teeth? Is your nose really shiny? Is your shirt looking rumpled?

Take the time to catch the little things so they don't become irrevocably big things after the fact.

Getting Familiar with Your Performance Space

During one of my training classes, one of the participants stepped in front of the camera to do his baseline performance. But he acted as if someone were shining a floodlight on him. He practically cowered under the bright studio lights. After a few minutes, he did adjust a bit, but during his entire presentation, he squinted like someone in desperate need of sunglasses. The sometimes-blazing lights are just one of the reasons why it is important to take the time to acclimate to the studio environment.

Find out where the director would like you to stand and take note of the way it is marked on the floor. Typically, the crew will have placed a piece of tape on the spot where they would like you to perform for the sake of proper framing and focus. And speaking of framing, make sure to ask the camera operator how you are being framed so you understand what sort of gestures will work and what will not.

If you haven't already done so, ask if you can practice reading your script off of the prompter. Don't just breeze through it quickly. Actually, read the entire script aloud to simulate how you will perform it.

You want to make sure that the lighting doesn't interfere with your ability to clearly see the words on the prompter.

The more time you spend getting familiar with your performance space, the more comfortable you should feel once it is time to record.

The Crew's Final Prep

While you are mentally preparing for your performance, the crew is also going through its own checklist. They are busy assessing the sound quality, making sure nothing could potentially interfere with the audio. They are adjusting the camera settings and tweaking the framing. They are looking for errant shadows or other lighting oddities.

Often, it feels like every single member of the crew is hyperfocused on you. It's enough to make anyone feel paranoid. But rest assured, you are more like a piece of furniture at that point. You are just one more thing in the shot, and the fact that you are living and breathing isn't of real consequence until the crew is ready to record. They are judging how the light is bouncing off you, not how eloquent you are sounding in rehearsal.

PULLING OFF A GREAT PERFORMANCE

All of your preparation has led up to this moment. The countdown is about to begin. But wait . . .

Three Last-Minute Reminders

- Remember when you determined who your ultimate viewer was for this piece? Bring that person to the fore and visualize him or her to help you establish the proper mental mind-set.
- Loosen yourself up through movement. Swing your arms. Take some deep breaths. If you are going to step into the shot, practice that move and be sure to land on your mark. A performance that starts stiff stays stiff. If you begin your performance by moving into the shot, you are much more likely to stay loose throughout.
- If you are not going to step into the shot, center yourself during the floor director's countdown by looking slightly down. Be ready to look up when he or she cues you to start.

TO SMILE OR NOT TO SMILE . . .

CASE STUDY

One of my clients came to me with a problem. She was hosting a video series for an external audience and was not happy with how she was coming across. This was a C-level executive who had impressive degrees and achievements to spare. She was certainly a master of her content with unquestionable credibility.

What was derailing her performance was the direction she was given right before every recording: *"Don't forget to smile."*

No doubt, looking dour is not a way to connect with your audience. However, not all on-camera performances call for a toothy grin. In this case, my client had a pleasant demeanor but was not an overly "smiley" person. Asking her to smile right before the red light went on was like asking her to balance on one leg. It felt uncomfortable and it showed. Her expression was more simpering than inviting. What's more, the video series was of a more serious nature, so a smile was incongruous with the content.

If someone tells you to be sure to smile, feel free to smile as you thank him or her for the reminder—and then decide if that direction matches the message. If the answer is yes, go for it. If the answer is no, then strive to be approachable and authoritative, but not inappropriately amused.

Stay Focused Despite Distractions

Once you are cued, you are officially "on." You may receive further affirmation of that fact by a red light ablaze on top of the camera called a tally light. Tally lights indicate what cameras are live at any given time. They are especially helpful when it is a multiple camera shoot.

In order to avoid being overwhelmed by the moment, try to stay focused on the meaning behind the words. Remember, you are there to deliver a really valuable message to your viewer, and you want to make sure they hear it and comprehend it the first time through.

Pay attention to your visual cues in your script, but if you accidentally skip over a pause or emphasize a word you had not intended to stress, do not let it throw you off. Keep the volume of your inner critic at a low-level hum and press on with the same amount of energy and intensity as you did from the beginning.

If your performance is not live, resist the urge to stop just because you think you may have said something incorrectly. You have several sets of eyes watching your performance, and if you mess something up, they will stop you. I have seen plenty of clean takes be disrupted abruptly by presenters who thought they had made a mistake—only to find out that they hadn't.

Periodically, something can go awry in the studio that has absolutely nothing to do with you. A light bulb can blow. Someone off camera may need a drink of water to stifle a tickle in his or her throat. This may cause a member of the crew to take action while you are still in the midst of your performance. Just like rubberneckers everywhere, you may have a strong desire to check out what's going on. But don't. Your viewer has no idea that a light bulb is being replaced to your left or that your camera operator is about to gag.

Your job is to focus only on the conversation you are having with your viewer. If the action is not in the frame, then it is of no consequence to you and certainly not to your audience.

THE REVOLVING CHAIR

CASE STUDY

Sometimes, even professionals don't realize the implications of their actions on the set. Such was the case for one of my more demanding on-camera spokesperson jobs.

I was hired to perform a series of videos, each about five minutes in length. The content was fairly dense with industry-specific vocabulary. What made it even more challenging was the fact that I needed to do what is called a "clean take" for each piece. In that case, perfection wasn't a "nice to have" it was a "*need* to have."

The shoot went well, and I was thrilled to be finishing up the project with the final video in the series. I was about three minutes into my performance when the camera operator who was doubling as the director got up from the swivel chair in which he had been sitting. The chair

(Continued)

(*Continued*)

was located about two feet away from the camera. At that point, and for reasons unknown, he started to slowly spin the chair in circles. Yes, it had been a long day for all of us, but was it really the right time to test how smoothly and rapidly the chair could revolve?

My inner critic is relatively well controlled, but she started to seethe. I did somehow manage to make it to the end of the take without a bump, but as soon as I was done, I allowed my inner critic to have a very outer voice.

"What were you thinking?!!" I asked not so politely.

The director apparently had been completely unaware of how distracting his basically absentminded actions were. He didn't even realize he was doing it. He was mortified and very apologetic. We all ended up laughing about it.

And for any subsequent jobs we have done together, there has been nary a swivel chair in sight.

The Most Dangerous Part of Your Performance

Presumably, you have practiced your script enough that you know when you are nearing the end. You may consider this time for celebration, but it actually is the portion of your performance where you need to focus the most.

The last 30 seconds of any on-camera performance are full of potential potholes. This section describes a few to avoid.

The Runaway Train Ramble

Even if you have carefully modulated the pace of your delivery for you entire performance, it is almost irresistible to not speed up at the end. You are *so* close.

But think about what that means for your viewers. So far, you have done everything in your power to tailor your message and its delivery to them. Picking up your pace does them a disservice.

Now is a time when your visual cues become even more valuable. You may not feel like pausing, but you know those marks are there for a reason. Rely on them to keep you on track.

Mentally Moving On

Just like a marathoner who trips 50 yards from the finish line, it is all too easy to allow your mind to look beyond the performance and already start celebrating. Unfortunately, that fleeting loss of focus can cause you to flub and force you to have to do another take.

You have already put in a yeoman's effort to get this far into your performance. See it through to the very end.

Stopping the Performance before the Real End

You may think your job is done as soon as you utter the last word of your script. Not true. You may have nothing left to say, but you have to sustain that connection with your audience until the crew indicates you are finished. They may say "cut" or "clear"—the terminology varies, but the point is that you should stay in your spot and maintain eye contact with your viewer until you are told the camera is no longer live.

Too often, novices do at least one of the following immediately after they say their final words:

- Their facial expressions dramatically shift to reflect how they felt about their performances. Often, negative thoughts manifest themselves as grimaces, eye rolls, or even projected tongues. (Totally true.)
- They look off camera as if asking if they are done or need to do it again.
- They make the decision for themselves that they are finished and walk quickly off the set.

Your words are only part of your performance. Your body language speaks volumes, too, and if you are advertising displeasure or uncertainty with the experience, your audience will read that easily.

If the performance is going to be edited, there is an even greater need to stay engaged until you are told. The editor will need a few seconds after your final words to either fade to black or cut to another piece of video. If you immediately let your guard down, make a face, or walk out of the shot, the editor will have to cut off your performance too abruptly. It will look and sound awkward. At a minimum, count "one-thousand-one, one-thousand-two" in your head to give your editor a bit of a buffer.

REVIEWING YOUR PERFORMANCE

Once your performance is complete, you may want to chalk it up to experience and never think about it again. However, that would be a lost opportunity for your personal growth.

Watching your on-camera work is one of the most valuable ways to develop as a performer. Take note of what you think you did well and what you might want to do differently next time around. And make sure there *is* a next time.

Any time someone asks if you would be willing to go on camera, give an enthusiastic "yes!" Performance jitters diminish with familiarity. In short, the more you perform on camera, the better a performer you will be.

CHAPTER TAKEAWAYS

- Corporate video should not be a visual white paper.
- Video is best at eliciting emotion, not conveying large volumes of information.
- Shorter videos stand a better chance of being watched in their entirety.
- Limit your uninterrupted facetime to no more than two-minute chunks.
- Create your content with the viewer in mind.
  - Organize for the ear with the Rule of Three.
  - Determine who your audience will be in order to pick the proper tone and level of detail.
  - Write the way you speak.
  - Add visual cues based on drawing out the meaning of each sentence.
- Practice, practice, practice.

- Choose your wardrobe that tends toward boring but matches audience expectations.
- Keep your cell phone out of the studio.
- Understand who is who in the studio crew:
  - Floor director
  - Audio technician
  - Camera operator
  - Teleprompter operator
- Check yourself in the mirror right before your performance.
- Allow yourself the time to acclimate to your performance space.
- Remember to visualize your viewer.
- Loosen yourself up immediately before show time.
- Stay focused throughout your performance despite distractions.
- As you near the end, force yourself to stay in the moment.
- Do not relax until the crew tells you "clear."
- Watch your performance afterward and look for what you did well and what you would like to do differently next time.

CHAPTER 13

Videoconferencing and Interviews via Video Chat

When I first thought about writing this book on communicating through the camera, my vision was rather narrow: I wanted to teach people how to handle presenting on camera in a *studio* setting. Fast-forward only a few years, and the focus of the book has widened exponentially. Cameras in the literal hands of the masses have democratized the use of video-enabled calls, conferences, and chat. "FaceTime" is now a verb. The "bloop" sound of Skype is almost as familiar as the voice of Siri.

Companies have clamored to acquire videoconferencing (VC) capabilities or have expanded their use of them. According to Andrew Davis of Wainhouse Research, "The bottom line is that VC is not just for meetings anymore, but, like voice, is rapidly becoming a mainstream communications tool for employees up and down the organization chart."[1]

However, just because you own the tool doesn't mean you can wield it well. You may have a circular saw in your garage, but that does not make you a furniture maker.

In this chapter, I will help you apply what you have learned thus far about communicating through a camera and will include best practices suggested by videoconferencing and Web chat pros to improve your virtual presence and performance.

CHANGES IN WHERE AND HOW YOU WORK

Work is no longer where you go, it is what you do.

Andrew Davis, Wainhouse Research

As anyone can attest by listening to the traffic reports around the country, there are still plenty of people who commute to work by car, train, or bus. But there are an increasing number of people whose commutes require navigating the halls of their own homes.

According to a report by Wainhouse Research, "more and more knowledge workers find that working from home, remote offices, or even public spaces provides them advantages in flexibility, downtime, and lower stress from commuting. As a by-product, companies are finding that many offices are empty very often."[2]

Consequently, if you can't round up your employees for a meeting on site in the corporate conference room, you switch to a virtual meeting model where users can join from the device of their choosing.

Primarily, that virtual meeting model is audio based only. In fact, according to Andrew Davis of Wainhouse Research, "More people are becoming comfortable with videoconferencing as a replacement for audio conferencing, but it's still got a long way to go."

That's welcome news for my colleague who has a weekly conference call at 5 A.M. with her counterparts in Europe, the Middle East, Africa (EMEA), and Asia-Pacific. While she has the option to turn on her webcam, she has absolutely no desire to do so. It's a lot easier to *sound* bright-eyed and bushy-tailed before dawn than it is to *look* that way. A voice-only call is a safer option than a video call where your pajamas would definitely be a no-no.

But a major shift in office demographics may change virtual-meeting expectations that could make teleconferencing seem almost as passé as a rotary phone.

MAKE WAY FOR MILLENNIALS

CASE STUDY

As a mom of two boys, I have historically been in charge of scheduling my children's playdates, a common phrase in parenting parlance that roughly translates to "friends getting together to socialize." If I were going to host, I knew in advance when my boys' buddies were going to be dropped off and picked up so I could make sure my house was neat and tidy for visitors—since young boys are *always* concerned about clutter. (Okay, so my obsessive-compulsive tendencies were a little misplaced.)

Today, my teenagers regularly invite guests into our abode, but I am often ambushed by their presence. In fact, I rarely hear their friends come in. Why? Because they don't come in through the door—they come in through a screen. The teenage version of a playdate is often held over FaceTime, Skype, or whatever video chat app they have at their disposal.

Usually, I have no problem with their friends virtually hanging out at our house, but it can be disconcerting if you are caught unawares. What if their buddies see that laundry that hasn't been put away! The horrors!

My boys are among a generation that has grown up communicating through cameras. Not only do they feel comfortable doing it, they expect to always be able to do it. And research bears that out.

(Continued)

(*Continued*)

Wainhouse Research compared the use of VC—both personal and professional—with employee age, and the trend is clear. The younger you are, the more likely you are to use VC to connect with friends and family *and* to conduct business, as you can see in the following figure. These digital natives are projected to make up 75 percent of the workforce by 2025.[3]

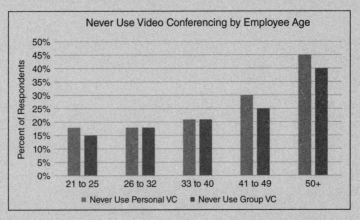

Source: Reproduced with permission of Andrew Davis, Wainhouse Research, LLC.

Millennials expect to be able to use VC or at least video chat, and if a company does not offer it, it will likely appear way behind the times. Companies will want to recruit the best graduates, and how they equip their employees to communicate may be a valuable tool in the talent war.

While the younger generation has a distinct advantage in terms of their level of comfort communicating through the camera, they are at risk of being almost *too* comfortable. What is appropriate for a casual FaceTime session may not be for a virtual video meeting with a colleague or client. Eating a piece of pizza while Web chatting with a friend? Just fine. Scarfing down leftover Chinese takeout while videoconferencing with the leadership team? Not so much.

HIRING BY SKYPE

Video chat and conferencing can be a hiring manager's dream. Finding the right person for the job is challenging enough, but the time required to do so can make it even more painful. VC can help alleviate both pain points.

More and more companies are opting to conduct their first round of interviews using VC tools, which are often enabled by cloud services. The reasons for the rise in this application are simple—it's a matter of dollars and *sense*.

Travel Cost Savings

Any hiring manager wants to cast as wide a net as possible for applicants, but often, that can be cost prohibitive. You can only fly so many people in without busting the budget. VC breaks down those geographic barriers. Instead of being limited to who is within driving distance, hiring managers can choose any solid applicant with an Internet connection.

Those first virtual interviews can screen out the "no thank yous" and narrow down the list of who warrants a face-to-face—at a much lower cost.

Fewer Scheduling Headaches

The logistical nightmare associated with the hiring process is real. Trying to coordinate the schedules of both the interviewer and the interviewees can make anyone reach for the Advil. It becomes even more complicated if more than one company representative wants to be present for the vetting process.

With VC, all parties only need to block out enough time for the meeting itself, not the travel to and from the interview site. Plus, they can come together virtually, no matter where they are physically. And let's say not everyone can actually make the meeting in real time. There's the added benefit that most VC can be recorded and reviewed at a more convenient time.

But hiring by Skype or any other video meeting tool isn't just a boon for the human resources department. According to PGi, a leading provider of collaboration software and services, 66 percent of the talent pool prefers to use video during the interview process.[4]

The bottom line: that empty slot is filled much faster at a lower cost to boot.

WHY YOU WANT TO TURN ON YOUR WEBCAM

One of my clients told me she is often a participant in VC, but she is never seen on camera. Why? She puts duct tape over the camera lens on her laptop. She has managed to fool her counterparts for months with the fabrication that her built-in camera is out of commission, preferring to remain a disembodied voice.

My client obviously does not buy into the benefits of actually making virtual meetings visual. However, allow me to offer a few points to ponder in support of using video when you conference:

- Participants stay engaged.

    If you want to get something done, you want people to focus on what is being discussed, not on everything *but*. People pay attention when they are always on camera. Checking e-mail, playing with the dog, ordering from the drive-thru while on mute—these all become much more difficult, if not impossible, when you are being held visually accountable.

    Perhaps Andrew Davis of Wainhouse Research says it best: "In business, I joke, if I'm having this conversation with you, I want to do it on video because you have to look into the camera and pretend you are interested in what I'm saying, whereas, if it's an audio call, I know you're doing your e-mail, you're cleaning your desk drawers, or whatever."

- Today's tools are better than yesterday's tools.

    Better mobile network bandwidth, more intuitive interfaces, and high-definition audio and video have made VC less of a gimmick and more of a go-to communication option. Older versions were often clunky, and sessions usually started with at least 10 minutes of confusion ("How do I connect?" "I can't hear you." "I can't see myself."). The majority of the new generation of VC tools actually deliver what they promise, which makes them much more attractive.

- You can actually read the virtual room.

    Our nonverbal communication can often speak louder than our verbal. If you want to know what someone thinks of your proposal, watch his or her facial expressions and overall body language. That feedback can be revealing and allow you to re-calibrate your delivery.

Still not convinced? You may have no choice.

"Videoconference usage is destined to increased," observes Davis, given the massive migration of millennials into the workforce. "Price and the performance continue to move in the right direction, and that makes videoconferencing far more feasible for many, many people."

BEST PRACTICES FOR VC

While there are still many organizations that have devoted VC rooms with built-in systems, this discussion will focus on best practices for video conferencing with BYOD—bring your own device—whether it is your laptop, your webcam, or your phone.

How effective you are at communicating through that camera is largely dependent on the how you prepare for and approach your videoconference or chat.

Technical Considerations

Brad Simmons is Program Manager for Leadership and Team Intelligence at Cisco, home of the Goliath of collaboration tools: WebEx. Over the course of his career, he's seen countless conferencing sessions, some done well and some not. Here are some of his suggestions for making sure your VC is a success:

- Become familiar with the interface in advance.

  Each vendor's products have different layouts, and some of them are more intuitive than others. Even within WebEx, there are a variety of versions and capabilities as a result. Simmons suggests you take a tip from VC pros: "The good ones always ask which version of WebEx are you using." Don't just wait until the last minute to dial in. If you encounter any issues, your colleagues (or clients) will not enjoy watching or listening to you troubleshoot.

- Choose your conference time wisely.

  There's only so much bandwidth available, and how much can be squeezed through it can be put to the test by the inclusion of video. You can experience a significant loss of quality in both audio and video due to compression. One way to mitigate its effects is to choose a time when Internet traffic is less. Simmons says folks on the East Coast should shoot for early morning when West Coasters are still asleep. Later in the afternoon is better for the West Coast as the East Coast starts to log off. Conversely, Simmons says videoconferences on Friday afternoons should be avoided at all costs. Everyone is rushing to wrap up work before the weekend.

■ Consider taking audio out of the equation when participating via laptop or desktop.

Remember, there is only so much you can send through the bandwidth and video gobbles up a lot of it. Brad suggests calling in using your smartphone and putting it on speaker phone if you want your best shot at keeping the video quality high.

■ Use the built-in speakers and microphone as a last resort.

Industry experts say videoconference attendees are much more forgiving of poor video quality than poor audio quality. While a call can continue without the visual, audio is the underpinning of the entire meeting. With that in mind, you should pay special attention to what audio option you exercise.

While built-in speakers and microphones on your laptop or smartphone might seem like the easiest option, they are usually on the lowest rung of the quality ladder. They're designed to fit into a small space, not to produce high fidelity. Their location is also a problem, according to Sara Mosely of HighFive, a VC vendor, "They are too close to the screen, so sound waves bounce off the display and cause a cluttered sound, which increases distortion and decreases clarity."[5]

Cisco's Simmons agrees and notes that every environment is different. Some rooms allow the sound to bounce around a lot more than others. Simmons suggests investing in a USB microphone or a headset. Headphones might mess up your hair but do provide the clearest audio, which allows you to hear the nuances of any conversation.

▪ Simplify your slide presentation.

Many VC tools allow users to share slides during the session. This may not involve how you appear on camera, but it certainly impacts how well you communicate during a videoconference.

Simmons warns against making slides too busy. When they are compressed, they may become distorted and difficult to read. Plus, some of those involved in the conferencing may be calling in on their mobile devices. Imagine trying to read a ton of text off a screen that size.

Setting Considerations

The importance of setting the stage for your VC performance is often undervalued, but overlooking the basics can have a serious impact on whether your message is heard or missed. (It will be hard for your audience to concentrate on what you're saying if they are wondering why you haven't folded that mountain of laundry in the background.)

Here are some suggestions on how to set yourself up for success:

▪ Make sure your background is clean and uncluttered.

You may be a slob at home, but you don't want to reveal that at work. VC opens the window of opportunity for that messiness to seep into your professional image.

Find a spot where the background is relatively free of distractions. Bookshelves on which items are neatly arranged can provide depth to the shot without overwhelming it. A potted plant positioned over your shoulder can soften the image, but make sure you won't look like it's growing out of your head.

Don't make the mistake of sitting directly in front of a blank wall. It can be too sterile and appear as if you are sitting in a jail cell or waiting for your passport photo to be taken.

▪ Control the lighting.

If you work from home, you may have your desk smack up against a wall with a window directly behind you. If you try to take part in a video meeting with that desk/window setup, you will likely look like you are in the witness protection program. With light from the window streaming in behind you, your entire body will be in silhouette.

Backlight is a big no-no when using VC. The camera will blow out the exterior light and bring everything else into shadow. You want to make sure you are lit from the front so your face is fully illuminated. That's where you want the focus to be. However, that's not without challenges.

Overhead lighting can cast nasty shadows on your facial features, obscuring your eyes, and eye contact is essential for connecting with your audience. Lighting from below can make you look like you are about to tell a scary ghost story around the campfire, and it certainly isn't flattering.

Ideally, you will be able to light yourself from the front but also have a way to light some of your background as well. You don't want to look like you are in a cave.

One of the best techniques is to use a desk lamp that will offer soft but ample light. Not all lamps are created equal though. Some wield too harsh a beam and wash you out. Find a wattage that works for your environment. Check out the shot in advance and experiment with different positions to find the one that doesn't cast awkward shadows. I usually have a combination of natural light from a nearby window with a desk lamp situated behind my screen.

 WARNING

Do not rely on your computer screen as your sole light source. You will look terrible. Trust me.

■ Put your camera in a comfortable position.

Ideally, you want your camera lens to be at eye level and at a distance far enough away to allow you to be seen at least from the shoulders up. If you are too close to the camera, your conversation partners will almost feel like you are invading their personal space. If you are too far away, you will appear removed from the discussion and look less engaged.

Pay attention to the angle of your camera. You don't want to be looking down unless you like to appear as if you have a double chin. You also don't want to position the camera too high or you will look like you are five years old, looking up at Santa.

Make sure anything you need to reference is within easy reach. Keep your notes handy so you don't have to move out of the screen. It can look odd when you disappear out of frame.

Performance Considerations

As with any on-camera performance, the MVPs also apply to video-conferences. You need to adjust your mental mind-set to focus on your audience. You need to pick your pace with your conversation partner in mind and remember to pause appropriately. And you need to be aware of how your framing will affect your freedom to gesture.

Here are some additional parameters of VC that you need to keep in mind if you want to truly use the tool well:

- Treat your videoconference as if you were meeting face to face.

   Even though you may be on the other side of the world from your conversation partner, for the time when you are on the call, you are in the same room. So your behavior should mirror how you would behave as if you were across the table from them, not across the globe.

   Pick a level of formality that matches what would be expected in person. You may be at home, but your approach should be office professional. Don't fidget. Don't slouch. Don't scratch that itch in a place that might be embarrassing.

   Above all, please, please don't eat. No one looks good scarfing down food on camera.

- Consider where you will look.

   As discussed in a previous chapter, videoconferences are a conundrum for eye contact. Most of us want to look at the face we see on the screen, which is usually the person with whom we are speaking, our conversation partner. However, by doing so, we are inadvertently avoiding eye contact, which takes away from the feel of a face-to-face meeting.

   Cisco's Brad Simmons explains the problem, "In your own head, you are talking to them, but to them (your conversation partner) it looks like you're talking to their chest."

   Brilliant minds have gone to work on this problem of imperfect eye contact, and some have actually come up with solutions. Some involve teleprompter-like devices that fit over the lenses of webcams, laptops, and tablets and allow you to have direct eye contact for web chats as well as actual prompting if desired. Software has also been developed that digitally changes the direction of your gaze to make you appear to be looking at your conversation partner, even though the camera is capturing you looking down. Even Apple has a patent for technology that would banish the separate, single lens, and instead, embed multiple sensors and lenses into the actual monitor.

Unfortunately, none of these solutions are readily available or, in the case of the prompter-like device, on the top of our must-buy lists.

So what do you do with the current configuration?

If it's just two of you on the call, force yourself to look at the lens as much as possible. Feel free to glance quickly at the screen if you want to detect a reaction to something you've said. However, the more you can artificially emulate that direct eye contact, the better.

If you have multiple people taking part in the conference, you can afford to look at the screen more often, but if you are speaking, try to speak directly to the lens. You words will have much more impact.

■ Beware of gesture lag.

As you have learned in previous chapters, movement is important to keep nerves in check and to avoid looking too stiff. However, if your gestures are too abrupt and frequent, they can appear to splay across the screen. Compression can cause a lag time in your movements and make them appear choppy and delayed. To minimize the effect, be purposeful in your gestures and err on the side of too few rather than too many.

Also, be aware of where your hands are relative to the camera. If you move them too close to the lens, they can easily overwhelm the shot and look giant.

■ Pick the proper chair.

You may appreciate the utility of a swivel chair, but shifting back and forth during VC can be a distracting to your fellow users. My suggestion is to sit in a chair that's comfortable but static. Your slight swivel may seem insignificant to you, but the camera will exaggerate the movement.

- Speak at normal volume.

    Provided you have chosen an adequate audio option, you do not need to project your voice to make yourself heard. Always check your sound in advance to make sure you are within range, but once the call starts, trust that your usual speaking volume will suffice. No one likes to be shouted at!

    By the same token, you don't want to whisper either. Depending on the sensitivity of your microphone, if you speak at too low a volume, you may end up not being heard well enough, and others participants might not tell you.

- Find a relatively quiet spot.

    The sound of a dog barking in the background during a conference call has become almost cliché, but it remains a common complaint. Even if your dog *never* barks, your pup is guaranteed to speak up at the worst possible moment. Find a way to keep him out of earshot if you can. Open windows leave open the possibility of noises you can't control: the garbage truck collecting the neighborhood trash, emergency sirens wailing or the cacophony of sounds created by the local landscaping crew. Audio interruptions once in a blue moon will be forgiven, but won't be forgotten if they happen on a regular basis.

- Don't try to show documents on a webcam.

    Cameras found on your phone, laptop, or webcam are not suitable for show and tell. If you want to share a written document during the videoconference, share it with the tool for screen or slide sharing. It will be nearly impossible for your audience to make it out if you hold it up, no matter how close you bring it to the camera. Take the time to upload it in advance so it's easily accessible and seen by all on the call.

RECORDING A VIDEOCONFERENCE

There are many options for recording a videoconference, no matter what VC software you use. With new ones coming on the market on a daily basis, a current list would be obsolete by the time the book goes to print. My suggestion is to do your research and try out several that appear most promising. The majority offer a trial period with some-times a less robust version, but it allows you to take it for a test drive for free.

No matter what application you choose, you can set yourself up for success by following these guidelines:

- Shut down applications you don't need.

     Running any sort of videoconference or Web chat applica-tion requires a lot of computer processing power. If you record that call, you will significantly up the ante. To lessen the load and reduce hiccups due to the strain on your system, shut down any applications that are not essential for the video call.

     The processing drain also provides another argument for using an external microphone during a videoconference. My usually silent laptop has a tendency to have its fans whir loudly to life when I record any virtual sessions on Skype or Google Hangouts. If I were to rely on the built-in microphone, my au-dio would sound like I was sitting in the middle of a windstorm.

- Make sure you have enough storage space.

     Recorded video calls can become monster-sized files. Make sure you have enough storage space available to contain them. Also, take note of where your recorded calls will be saved. Dif-ferent applications have different default settings. You want to make sure you can track them down when you need them.

- Turn off notifications.

     If you are planning to record the call to be able to show it to others, change the settings in any applications that send you notifications. Imagine you are recording a stellar interview and suddenly a pop up window blares that you've received a 40 per-cent off coupon from Gap. Exciting perhaps for you, but not for the person who is watching the recorded version of the inter-view. Not only does it look highly unprofessional, but you also run the risk of having personal information revealed. (Does your colleague really need to know you have an appointment at your OB/GYN?)

     Shut those notifications down during the video call and feel free to turn them back on afterward.

■ Watch out for audio feedback.

You may need to make some adjustments to your setup if your microphone is getting feedback or an echo from your speakers. If you are using an external microphone, try moving it further away from your speakers. You can also try turning down the volume of your speakers' output. The foolproof way is to use headphones or a headset.

 Exercise for VC Best Practices

ACTIVITY

This exercise will allow you to test out the videoconference best practices outlined in this chapter at a time when the stakes are low.

You will need a friend who is willing to spend some time chatting with you via video through an application you both have on your devices.

WHAT YOU WILL NEED TO COMPLETE THIS EXERCISE

- A device with video chat capabilities:
  - Webcam connected to a desktop
  - Smartphone
  - Tablet
- A video chat application such as Skype, Google Hangouts, FaceTime, or ooVOO
- An external application for recording video calls such as eCamm Call Recorder for Skype or Camtasia for Google Hangouts

SCENARIO

Establish a time to video chat with a friend or family member. You do not need to worry about content. This exercise is all about performance and raising your self-awareness of how you look and sound during a videoconference.

WHAT TO DO BEFORE THE CALL

Give yourself enough time to do the preparation necessary to increase your chances of having a successful call.

- Prepare your computer by shutting down extraneous application and turning off notifications.

(Continued)

(Continued)

- Check your audio. Each VC application has its own method for doing so. Follow its suggested technique and adjust your equipment if necessary.
- Check your video. If you identify anything in the background that might be distracting, remove it. If you can't take it out of the shot or you can't find a better background, you can hang a sheet over it to at least minimize the distraction.
- Position the camera at the appropriate angle, sit squarely in the frame and dial away.

WHAT TO DO DURING THE CALL

Once you have established a connection with your conversation partner, start recording your call.

Engage in casual conversation and take note of the following:

- Is the audio clean and clear on both ends?
- Is there any feedback resulting from the sound emitting from the speakers bleeding into the microphone input? If so, adjust the position of your microphone and see if you can mitigate it.
- Ask your conversation partner if there is anything in your frame that might be distracting. Conversely, assess his or her background for potential problems. Identifying issues on the other end will help you to avoid them as well.
- Experiment with eye contact. Try speaking to the screen, which shows your conversation partner, and then try speaking directly to the lens. Ask if he or she could detect a difference.
- Ask your conversation partner to do the same and see the difference for yourself.
- Test the limits of your gesturing capabilities. Vary your movement to see if there is a lag. Move your hands toward the lens and ask your conversation partner to identify when the gestures appear intrusive.
- Try sharing your screen. Each application has a different way to do so. Practice toggling back and forth between the screen share mode and you on camera. (Some applications allow you

to do both at the same time. Find out what the capabilities are in advance.)

PLAYING IT BACK: CRITIQUING YOUR PERFORMANCE

Often, the best way to assess how you come across is by watching a recording of your performance. Obviously, this exercise was less formal than your previous ones, but it is worth reviewing to cement the key learnings.

If you were not happy with the clarity of your audio, consider investing in some new equipment to improve your sound. If you found the imprecise eye contact annoying, perhaps pick up one of the teleprompter-like overlays for your laptop or webcam which makes maintaining perfect eye contact a breeze.

Once you have made yourself aware of trouble spots—both potential and real—ask your friend or family member to engage in one more videoconference to see if your adjustments made a difference. Record it again so you can compare and contrast the before and after calls.

CHAPTER TAKEAWAYS

- Videoconferencing is becoming a mainstream communication tool across the enterprise with many users participating with their own devices.
- Its popularity is increasing as the workforce globalizes and spends less time within the confines of the corporate office.
- Millennials are digital natives who not only are comfortable with video chat but also expect to be able to use it.
- Human resources departments are using video chat more often as a way to conduct the first round of interviews for new positions.
- Videoconferencing holds people accountable by minimizing multi-tasking and allows participants to read nonverbal communication.
- Before a videoconference, learn the interface and test your audio and video quality.

- Keep your background clean and uncluttered.
- Control the lighting.
- Minimize audio interruptions.
- Consider when you should look at the camera lens and when you should look at the screen to read body language.
- Speak at normal volume.
- If you plan to record the call, prepare your computer for the heavy processing load.

NOTES

1. Andrew Davis, "Critical Issues Facing Collaboration Planners & IT Decision Makers: Making Video Conferencing a Multi-faceted Resource and Differentiator." http://blog.pinnaca.com/whitepaper-critical-issues-facing-planners-it-decision0makers, November 2015.

2. Andrew Davis, "Critical Issues Facing Collaboration Planners & IT Decision Makers: Workplace Trends Affecting Enterprise Communications Strategies." http://blog.pinnaca.com/whitepaper-critical-issues-facing-planners-it-decision-makers-part-vii, May 2016.

3. *Facing the Millennial Wave*, http://www.cushmanwakefield.com/en/research-and-insight/2014/facing-the-millennial-wave/.

4. Carlye Creel, "7 Must-Know Video Conferencing Statistics." July 3, 2014. http://blog.pgi.com/2014/07/7-statistics-video-conferencing/.

5. Sara Mosely, "The Reason Your Laptop Speakers Suck and How to Fix It." Highfive.com blog. September 2, 2016. https://highfive.com/blog/5-headphones-best-video-conferencing-audio-quality/.

CHAPTER 14

Webcasts—Best Practices for Panelists and Moderators

The bulk of this book has been devoted to on-camera performance, based on the application of the MVPs of performance success. While those tenets of the MVPs do still matter during a webcast, they diminish a bit in their importance. Why? When it comes to performing well in a webcast, the focus is on your expertise, not your performance prowess.

If you've been asked to be part of a panel discussion that will be broadcast—either live or live to tape—you presumably provide value, based on your knowledge and experience. That's what landed you on that panel in the first place. The fact that you are a solid on-camera presenter is a bonus, not the reason for your selection.

In this chapter, I provide some guidance on how to wow in a webcast, whether you are serving as a panelist or a moderator.

WHY A WEBCAST IS EASIER TO MASTER

Congratulations! You have been asked to be part of a webcast to share what you know with the masses. While the goals of webcasts vary, your participation in it indicates that you have been deemed either an expert in your industry, vertical, or field or considered to be a representative voice, more than capable of speaking to the topic at hand.

Sharing your expertise is right in your wheelhouse. After all, you are certainly master of your content. You've got this.

But then you show up at the studio on the day of the webcast, and your confidence begins to drain. The studio where it is being shot is cavernous and full of unfamiliar equipment. There are lots of people scurrying around preparing for what now feels like a much bigger deal than you anticipated. And then, you are told to report to "makeup."

Are you part of a webcast or a televised daytime talk show? Either way, you are feeling way out of your element.

It's easy to be overwhelmed by the webcast environment if it is not one where you normally work. The good news is a webcast is much easier to manage than any other on camera scenario, mainly because you are not in it alone. One of the most challenging aspects of communicating through the camera is the lack of feedback. During a webcast, you actually have other people with whom you can interact. They can nod their approval, voice their disagreement, or laugh at your jokes. Rather than a monologue, a webcast is a dialogue, complete with actual eye contact with others, unimpeded by a camera lens.

COFFEE TALK

CASE STUDY

For over a decade, I have been a regular webcast host for a corporate client with a very impressive production presence. They actually boast two giant studios with the latest equipment, and they use them regularly for both internal and external videos.

Many of the webcasts I have hosted over the years take place on what is called "the coffee table set." It is aptly named because the centerpiece of that set is an actual low-slung, oval-shaped table. Chairs hug one side of it, the number reflecting how many panelists are scheduled to appear, and one chair sits at the head of the table where the moderator sits. The other side of the table is bereft of chairs but fully occupied by three large cameras, each capturing different shots and angles.

This set provides a literal and figurative metaphor for what a good webcast should feel like: a conversation around a coffee table, hopefully an animated and interesting one. A successful webcast should consist of a fascinating dialogue with participants all offering a different point of view. The discussion shouldn't be restricted to a particular course but be free to follow down whatever path the participants decide to take it. It should feel spontaneous, not scripted.

But as you learned in Chapter 2, "Why the Camera Changes Everything," the mere presence of a camera in the room causes seismic shifts in the environment that deeply affect those in it. In the case of a webcast, there are usually three cameras—three times the trouble.

I have seen verbose panelists clam up as soon as the red light goes on. I have also seen normally restrained industry leaders launch into soliloquies, with nary a glance at their fellow panelists, because they thought the presence of a camera called for a grand performance.

What they did not understand was that cameras do not call for any special treatment—in fact, quite the opposite.

(Continued)

(*Continued*)

In a webcast, the cameras simply represent other people who are sitting at the table with you. They may not physically be on set, but they are eager observers who are hoping to be privy to some lively discourse. They are not tuning in to watch a TED Talk.

The best webcasts I have hosted on the coffee table set have been light on script and heavy on interaction. Even if the panelists might have had butterflies initially, once the conversation started rolling, they practically forgot the cameras were even there. They were totally immersed in what was being discussed. The fact that it was all being caught on tape and broadcast to thousands did not even show up on their radar. And that's just how it should be.

The less you think about the cameras, the more engaging and authentic the webcast will be. You actually have people on set with you to play off of, so you should leverage that for all it's worth. Feed off their feedback. Build upon their points and prod other panelists to weigh in. Pretty soon, the cameras will become an afterthought—a voyeur to a dynamic conversation.

BEST PRACTICES FOR PANELISTS

Spontaneity is the secret sauce for any webcast, but that does not mean a little planning and insider's knowledge is off-limits for webcast panelists. Allow me to share a few tips on how to be at your best when appearing as a webcast panelist.

Prepare Your Points

The producer of the webcast most likely chose you to fill a certain role, whether it is "domain expert" or "happy customer." It is up to you to find out what sort of insight he or she is hoping you will provide. Here are some key questions to ask:

- What is the focus of the webcast?
- What topics or concepts would you like me to address?
- Who else will be appearing on the panel? (It will give you a better idea of how you fit into the assembled group.)

- Will you have prepared questions, and if so, will I see them in advance?
- Will I be fielding questions from the audience (if it is live)?
- How long do you expect the webcast to run?

Once you have those basic questions answered, gather whatever materials you need and review them so the information will be fresh in your mind. Remember, an on-camera presentation is not the place for a data dump, so consider what points would be the most impactful.

Put some thought into the messages you want to convey. Jot down some talking points, but do not try to memorize specific wording. Memorization is the enemy of spontaneity. Trust yourself to communicate the concepts in whatever words come to you in the moment.

Plan Your Wardrobe

You've already learned about the basics of what works and what does not on camera, but here are a few additional considerations:

- Find out if your whole body will be in view or if you will be seen just from the waist up. Allow that to dictate what you pull from your closet.
- Find out what color the background is. If the backdrop is sky blue, you don't want to wear a sky blue shirt.
- Pick out several camera-friendly outfits and take them to the studio. Your producer will appreciate being able to select the best option relative to what other panelists are wearing.
- Ask the producer whether there will be a makeup artist available, so you will know whether you should arrive fully "done" or you can cede that job to a professional.

Refer to the chapters in Section Three of this book for specific advice on wardrobe, hair, and makeup.

Take Advantage of Rehearsal Time

If the studio is unfamiliar, always take the time to orient yourself to the set prior to the actual webcast. Sit in the chairs. Acclimate to the bright lights. Take note of any cables that may pose tripping hazards and result in a less-than-graceful moment.

Typically, there will be a short rehearsal prior to the live webcast. The purpose is mainly to practice the flow of the show, rather than run through the content. The crew will want to test out the transitions from one camera shot to the next. The producer will want the moderator to practice introductions and tosses to breaks.

As a panelist, you may be asked to start answering a question, but you will often be cut off pretty quickly. It may seem rude, but it serves two purposes. First, it saves time. The producer assumes you know what you are talking about and having you run through it seems like an unnecessary duplication of efforts. Second, it keeps the content fresh and keeps you from sounding overly rehearsed.

The real value of the rehearsal for you is that you will have a much better understanding of the webcast structure and what you will be contributing within that framework. If you've done your homework, you probably have identified some real pearls of wisdom you'd like to share. Use the rehearsal to figure out the best place within the webcast to say them.

Focus on the Action

Once the webcast begins, your world shrinks. The set may not take up much physical space within the studio itself, but once the show begins, your focus needs to stay within the confines of those directly involved in the conversation: the moderator, the panelists, and the silent observers represented by the cameras.

This may seem like an easy task, but distractions in the studio can have a strong gravitational pull. In your peripheral vision, you may detect a member of the crew moving with purpose toward something just off the set. You will desperately want to take a look to see what's up, but don't give in to the urge. Your viewers don't know someone is just to your left, fiddling with the light. Moreover, they don't care, so you shouldn't either.

Your job is to stay connected to what's happening on the set, to the exclusion of everything else. Once the red light flashes, the webcast action is all that matters until that red light goes off and the floor director says "clear."

Where You Should Look

Every time I moderate a webcast, I am asked the same question by at least one of the panelists: "Where should I look?"

This is a reasonable query, since a typical webcast will involve multiple cameras. How do you know which camera is the right one to address? Should you even be looking into the camera in the first place? The short answer is: it depends.

You could rely on the tally lights, those red beacons that blaze above the lens indicating which camera is live. But the fact that the tally light is on does not mean the director wants you to look into the camera. Sometimes, the director is trying to get a cutaway shot, which is designed to capture reaction to what is being said. Looking into the camera will make you look out of sync with the action on the set. So what do you do?

Here are some general guidelines for three common webcast situations.

When Someone Asks You a Question

The rule for this echoes what your mother probably told you. If someone asks you a question, look him or her in the eye when you answer. It looks natural and the converse would be quite rude.

Imagine you are meeting someone for the first time and he or she asks you what you do for a living. Rather than looking at that person when answering, you instead look in a totally different direction, never making eye contact. What a snob!

Sometimes, a panelist will be so obsessed with the presence of the cameras that he or she will forget good manners. And that's what it really boils down to. If someone asks you a question on set, you start to answer while looking at that person. However, if there are other people on the set, you may want to make them feel included as well, so you may look at the other panelists, too.

If your answer is long enough, you may even want to acknowledge the silent participants at home. A glance to the camera, not a full-bore stare, can also be effective.

When Presenting Uninterrupted to Viewers

Sometimes, a panelist will be asked to do a brief presentation within the webcast that is primarily directed to the audience on the other side of the lens. The presentation may include a series of slides and is designed to be delivered uninterrupted.

In this scenario, you will likely be introduced by the moderator who will hand you the baton. The best bet is to acknowledge the moderator by looking him or her in the eye (as your mother would advocate) and then transition to looking at the camera.

But which camera?

If you have a floor director, you are all set. He or she will point you to the right camera—or wave vigorously if you are looking at the wrong one to correct your course. However, not all webcasts will have a floor director.

Most webcasts are multicamera shoots. If the webcast is using three cameras, there will usually be one camera devoted to capturing the moderator. Another camera will capture the panelists while they are speaking. The third camera is often reserved for cutaways, or reaction shots.

If you are going to be addressing the viewing audience for longer than a minute or so, the director will likely want to frame you in a tight shot. In this case, the tally light will be a pretty reliable guide as will the position of the cameras. If you are looking over your shoulder, you are probably looking into the wrong lens. If you have two cameras in front of you, look for the light.

Deliver your presentation in its entirety directly to camera and then transition back to the moderator at the end by looking back at him or her. It is a visual passing of the baton, which your director will recognize and react to accordingly by either switching to a shot including the rest of the webcast participants or to a shot of the moderator, who will move the webcast along.

When Others Are Speaking

One of the biggest gaffes I see panelists make on webcasts is assuming they are not on camera as long as they are not speaking. Unless you know someone is going to do a solo presentation for a prolonged period of time, you are at risk of popping up on camera at any time during a webcast.

Throughout a webcast, the director will intersperse cutaway shots to create visual interest and capture reactions from panelists. All too often, I have seen panelists taken unawares and look completely disconnected from the action on the set. A panelist will be staring off into space, looking at his shoes or checking her watch. Not the enthusiastic reactions the director was hoping to televise, but cutaways come without warning and participants don't always cooperate.

To save you from looking ridiculous and to save the director from fits of frustration, stay engaged in the conversation on the set. Look at whoever is speaking and listen intently. A good moderator will prompt others to respond, and you do not want to be zoning out if you are asked to weigh in.

Until the webcast is over, consider yourself to be on camera and force yourself to be on your best behavior.

Opting Out of Using a Teleprompter

While it may be tempting to use a teleprompter for your webcast, as a panelist, don't succumb to the promise of perfect delivery. Even if you aced the chapter on tackling the teleprompter, a webcast is not the scenario in which to flex those muscles.

Webcasts are all about free-flowing dialogue. Teleprompter copy is rigid, and trying to switch back and forth between reading off the prompter and ad-libbing is challenging, even for the pros. Also, the audience will always be able to tell when you are reading versus when you are speaking off the cuff. The differences might be subtle, but they will be noticeable enough to diminish your authenticity. It's especially pronounced when only one panelist insists on using the teleprompter. It stifles spontaneous conversation because participants feel like they can't interject or go off script.

If you can't stomach the idea of going out on set empty-handed, you can always use notes. I wouldn't suggest plopping a legal pad on your lap, but a few inconspicuous cue cards featuring a few stats that you want to reference is not a big deal. Do not try to write out possible responses word for word. You won't be able to write them big enough to be seen on set anyway. Instead, jot down a few things that you definitely want to include but are afraid you might forget in the moment. Remember, brain cramps love specifics so write down names or numbers that might temporarily escape you.

Handling the Unexpected Question

You may have done everything right to prepare for your webcast debut. You found out what topics were going to be covered in advance, gathered all appropriate information, and put some thought into what points you were going to make. But a webcast, in essence, is live TV, and it is always a good idea to expect the unexpected—like a question that you have absolutely no idea how to answer.

The question may have come from the moderator, who probably posed it out of curiosity, not as a way to throw you. Many webcasts also incorporate questions from the live audience that are sent in through whatever webcast hosting service is being used. Sometimes, those questions are vetted before being passed on to the moderator to pose during the live show, but that vetting isn't foolproof.

When you are given a real stumper, your inner critic may start to wail: "You're on this panel because you are an expert. Why can't you answer this question?" You can almost feel your face turning red.

Your first impetus may be to try to answer the question as best you can, but you are treading on dangerous ground. While the webcast may be live, it will likely be recorded, archived, and accessible long after the actual event. You do not want your less-than-factual response to be played over and over again. Talk about a credibility buster.

It is perfectly fine to admit you don't know the answer. You aren't omniscient. If the moderator posed the question, be honest and say you would have to do more research before answering. If the question came from a viewer, take the same tack but offer to follow up after the webcast once you have had a chance to find out the answer.

BEST PRACTICES FOR MODERATORS

The role of the moderator is critical in the success or failure of a webcast. A good one can effortlessly lead panelists through a scintillating discussion and somehow makes it all flow together seamlessly. A bad one can make everyone involved look terrible with disjointed Q&A, lackluster enthusiasm, and pauses that are simply pregnant, not powerful.

Allow me to shed some light on how you can shine as a webcast moderator.

Directing the Conversation

Have you ever watched a panel discussion where the moderator's questions are longer than the panelists' responses? The moderator seems intent on showing just how very knowledgeable he or she is on the given subject and apparently is in love with the sound of his or her own voice. This shows a gross violation of the number one rule for moderators: listening is more important than speaking.

Your job is to direct the conversation, not dominate it. Hopefully, the panel is made up of truly fascinating experts who have unique perspectives on the topic at hand. It's up to you to put all of that collective wisdom on display by encouraging them to talk and interact with each other. Your role is to encourage conversation, not to take it over.

Preparing to Be a Moderator

As a moderator, you should not only research the topic being discussed but also do your homework on those who will be appearing on the panel with you.

You are not there as an expert, so you shouldn't try to learn everything there is to know on the subject. However, you want to have a broad enough understanding that you will be able to follow along and ask relevant questions.

You also want to acquaint yourself with the backgrounds and areas of expertise of the panelists. Understanding what each panelist brings to the table will help you guide the dialogue, so each person will have a chance to shine. Plus, if you are fielding questions from the webcast audience, you want to be able to direct that question to the panelist best suited to answer it. Let's say you are moderating a panel of analytics experts. If a viewer asks a question about analytics in elementary education, you don't want to ask the expert on analytics for financial fraud to weigh in.

Encouraging the Conversation

As a moderator, consider yourself the pilot of the webcast. Even though you may get suggestions from air traffic controllers (the producer and/or director) you're the one metaphorically flying the plane, steering the course of the webcast. It's a big responsibility that requires you to have that view from 10,000 feet.

Thanks to your preparation, you have a pretty good sense of what needs to be covered in the webcast and the role each panelist will likely play. Your job is to get from point A to point B with a show that is informative and entertaining enough that your audience sticks around.

Before the webcast begins, give your panelists warning that you will be encouraging them to interact with each other throughout. Once they have been put on notice, feel free to put that plan into action.

You may have a list of prepared questions, but don't feel that you can't insert your own. If *you* are curious, your audience probably is as well. If one panelist says something that you think might run counter to what another panelist thinks, press for that opposing voice to be heard. Ask open-ended questions, like "do you have anything to add?" Panelists will appreciate the opportunity to chime in, on their terms.

The only way you can recognize when to prod panelists for more is to actually listen to them intently. Often, moderators are too busy thinking about what question he or she is going to ask next, and miss opportunities to ask those follow-up questions that could add real value to the discussion.

Depending on the personalities of the panelists, there are times when a lively conversation becomes an out-of-control ramble that goes way off topic. At that point, it is also your job, as the moderator, to corral that conversation and steer it back on course. Wait for a break in the action and transition by quickly wrapping up that point and redirecting with a question dealing with a desired topic.

Don't let one panelist monopolize the conversation. As a moderator, you should keep casual track of how much airtime each panelist is receiving and seek to give fair play to all. If one person consistently talks over everyone else, it's your job to skillfully cut in and redirect the question so others can offer their insights.

Being the Ultimate Editor

How scripted a webcast is varies widely. Some may include a simple introduction of the topic and panelists, a list of proposed questions, and a close. Some may be heavily scripted affairs that leave little room for unplanned interaction.

The majority of the webcasts I host are most in line with the former. The copy for the webcast introduction and closing remarks is in the teleprompter. The questions are usually in there as well, but I do not rely on them because the way a conversation is predicted to flow is rarely the way it does during the "live" webcast.

The questions may be lined up in a logical fashion, but your guests may not have committed that order to memory. If you ask question 1, they may answer it but also cover questions 6 and 7 as well. And that's totally fine.

What is *not* fine is if you move through your list of questions and proceed to ask question 6 as if it hasn't already been addressed. Your panelists will probably stare back at you with confusion or annoyance, and you will feel like a dunce.

As the moderator, you are the last line of defense in protecting the integrity of the webcast. You are the ultimate editor. It's your job to catch any potential redundancies in content and to be flexible enough to edit on the fly. Your producer may pick up the potential problem in advance, but understand that he or she could also be vetting audience questions, giving instructions to the director, or doing myriad other things that happen behind the scenes during a show.

If a question has already been answered, skip it and move on to the next, even if it is sitting there in the prompter, waiting to be read. You can explain why you didn't read it after the show, and all involved will thank you for it.

▶ **WARNING**

Always bring a pen and hard copy—an actual paper version of your teleprompter script—to the set with you. You will want to work off a list of questions as you move through the webcast, marking off the ones that have been covered. The hard copy also serves as a vital backup in the event the teleprompter conks out.

STAYING HYDRATED

Anxiety around presenting on camera can cause dry mouth, that cottony sensation that makes you feel like you've been sucking on gauze. Webcasts can exacerbate the problem due to their length. Even if you're not prone to dry mouth, talking for up to an hour can leave anyone parched.

If the set allows, keep a glass of water with no ice within arm's reach. Feel free to take sips throughout the webcast, but preferably do so when you are not on camera. A skillful moderator will not ask you a question if he or she sees you taking a quick drink. If you are the moderator, grab a quick sip after you've asked a panelist a question.

MARCO RUBIO'S INFAMOUS DRY-MOUTH DEBACLE

CASE STUDY

In 2013, Senator Marco Rubio (R-FL) delivered the GOP rebuttal immediately following the State of the Union address. The nationally televised speech was a huge opportunity for the rising star in the Republican Party, but instead of being a shining moment, it became fodder for late-night parody.

Viewers could see Senator Rubio was struggling about halfway through his speech, his delivery sounding mushy as if his tongue had unexpectedly thickened. He licked his lips repeatedly, eventually touching them before finally reaching over to retrieve a very small plastic water bottle off camera. He took the tiniest of drinks and soldiered on, but he continued to periodically lick his lips.[1]

It was a very human moment, made awkward by his approach. Instead of just excusing himself and taking a drink that might actually have made a difference, Senator Rubio appeared almost as if he was being held captive by the camera. He lunged to the side rather than turning toward the stool where the water sat, not daring to break eye contact with the camera for more than a second.

There's no shame in experiencing dry mouth. Most of us will at one point or another, but Senator Rubio supplies a cautionary tale, according to Ian Crouch of *The New Yorker*, who offered this commentary the day after the speech: "At the very least, Rubio has given the political world a teaching moment: position a tall, clear glass of water on an easily accessible flat surface near the politician. Remind said politician to drink from it, if absolutely necessary, in a calm and resolute manner."[2]

Good advice for us all.

CHAPTER TAKEAWAYS

- A webcast is one of the easiest on-camera scenarios to master because you have people to play off of.
- A webcast should feel like a lively conversation around a coffee or dinner table.
- The cameras represent other people seated at the table.
- Panelists should not use a teleprompter. Webcasts thrive on spontaneity.
- Force yourself to focus on the action on the set from start to finish.
- Don't tune out just because you aren't speaking.
- Listening is more important for moderators than speaking.
- Moderators should direct the conversation, not dominate it.
- Moderators need to be flexible and ready to edit on the fly.
- Stay hydrated during a long webcast to avoid dry mouth.

NOTES

1. Any YouTube search will yield countless versions of the event. Here's one free of parody, auto-tune, or play-by-play commentary: https://www.youtube.com/watch?v=19ZxJVnM5Gs.
2. Ian Crouch, "Marco Rubio's Water Bottle Moment." NewYorker.com, February 13, 2013. http://www.newyorker.com/news/news-desk/marco-rubios-water-bottle-moment.

CHAPTER 15

Broadcast Interview Basics

The focus of this book is not *media training*, and that's by design. There are plenty of tomes available that do just that—some good, some terrible. What I wanted this book to primarily address was what I considered an unmet need: how to communicate well through a camera, *any* camera, not just one held by a journalist.

That being said, not including anything about broadcast interviews would leave a hole in your foundational knowledge that would bug me—and you, if suddenly the *Today* show calls requesting an interview.

Typically, there is very little lead time for a TV interview, certainly not enough time to read an entire book or to take a class on media training. Consider this chapter a crash course in broadcast interview best practices: what to do before, during, and after the event.

BEFORE THE TV INTERVIEW

Perhaps I should have added another section called "Decide if You Even Want to *Grant* the Interview" because that is the most important and first step to take. When giving a presentation, you should always analyze your audience. When asked for an interview, you should always analyze the reporter and the media outlet making the request before saying "yes."

While some may argue that all publicity is good publicity, I would advocate a more prudent approach. Not all media outlets are created equal, and you have to decide whether you or your brand want to be associated with theirs. The same holds true for the reporter who is making the request on behalf of that outlet. Someone who is known for "gotcha journalism" is someone you probably want to avoid. However, if someone who has a reputation for being fair wants to interview you, you may decide to proceed.

REPORTER AS FRIEND OR FOE

CASE STUDY

When I was a TV reporter, I was not a member of our station's I-Team, our award-winning investigative arm. They did amazing work, but frankly, I was not cut out for it. The one investigative piece I did early in my career gave me indigestion.

The focus of that story was on a minister who allegedly bilked some of his church members out of millions of dollars. There were other allegations of impropriety as well. After doing hours and hours of interviews with his accusers, following up on leads and combing through a seriously warped paper trail, I thought I was all in to finally expose this guy.

My videographer and I were staking out his church one day, and I saw the minister arrive. But he was not alone. His wife and teenaged children were with him.

I knew this guy was in all likelihood a very flawed person who had done a lot of damage. My story would bring much of that to light, but I couldn't help thinking about how the press coverage would impact his children, who probably didn't know of their dad's misdeeds.

The station did air the story, and it was well received. However, I knew this kind of work was not what I wanted to do. Was I simply too nice? Maybe I saw too many shades of gray? All I knew for sure was that I did not enjoy digging up dirt, even if it definitely deserved every shovel full.

My distaste for heavy investigative work of the I-Team ilk did not mean I only did fluff stories. I could cover both general assignment and spots news (breaking stories) with the best of them, but I was not going to be the one who ambush-interviewed someone as he or she was leaving home, even if that person was a convicted slimeball.

Reporters do not all follow the same moral compass, nor do all media outlets expect their news gatherers to adhere to a high standard of media ethics. (In some cases, "media ethics" is an oxymoron.)

If a reporter asks you for an interview, you need to know what that reporter's typical method of operation is. Are you saying "yes" to a reporter who will give you a fair shake, or are you saying "yes" to a reporter who won't think twice about quoting you out of context if it makes for a better story? You need to find out before accepting the invitation, and even then, proceed with caution.

Find Out the Focus

Once you have agreed to the interview, it is your job to become the interviewer yourself. Find out as much as you can about the story's focus, angle, and your role in it. If the interview request stems from a particular incident or event, you may already know the focus, and perhaps the wheels of crisis communications management are already in motion. But if that's not the case, try to learn as much as you can about why you are being interviewed, so you can prepare appropriately.

You can ask for a list of questions, but don't be surprised if you don't receive one. Some news outlets have a policy that their reporters never give out a list of questions in advance. However, some reporters simply may not have one. When I conduct interviews, I have a general idea of the topics I want to discuss, but I don't have questions lined up, ready to be tossed out one after another. I prefer to let the conversation follow a natural course and peel back the layers of the story in real time. If I hear something worth probing, I do—and likely uncover something that I wouldn't have if I had stuck to a prescribed path.

You will probably have more luck if you ask for the topics that will be discussed during the interview. The reporter should have no problem doing that, but if he or she does, be wary.

Simplify Your Talking Points

Any media trainer will advise you to create talking points that you can stick to during an interview. There is merit to this process, but only if it doesn't come across as overly polished, insincere, or too self-promoting. The story is not a commercial, so a shameless plug is just that—shameless—and will probably not make air.

Once you have figured out what the focus will be, fall back to the Rule of Three and identify three main messages you'd like to impart. In broadcast, brevity rules, so anything beyond three points will take up too much time.

You may have three main messages, but you can articulate them in different ways. In fact, trying to memorize specific wording will only result in your sounding artificial and robotic. Think about how you can articulate your chosen themes using analogies or examples that will convey a lot of meaning concisely.

Speak jargon-free. Unless the story will be broadcast through a narrow channel, you need to simplify your language for a general audience. Test your talking points with people outside of your field of expertise to make sure they are easily understood.

Seek to Speak in Sound Bites

Now that you know *what* you want to say, let's talk about *how* you want to say it. If you'd like your fully formed thought to remain intact, shoot for saying it in 15 seconds or less, which will make it an attractive option for a sound bite. If you think that time frame sounds ridiculous, consider this: In 2011, the average length of a sound bite in broadcast news stories was 9 seconds, so that 15-second suggestion is actually generous.[1]

 NOTE

A *sound bite* is a small excerpt pulled from a longer recorded interview that is inserted into a broadcast news story.

In order to effectively get your message across, you need to be aware of these time constraints and adapt to them accordingly. If you are completely confounded, let me give you some tips.

- Don't bury the lead. Put your most important information first so if you are cut off, you will have already said what really matters.
- If you are there to provide your expert opinion, don't simply state facts. The reporter can do that. Instead, provide context for those facts that will move the story along.
- Resist the urge to expound. Once you have succinctly answered the question, stop. Leave it up to the reporter to ask for more.

Practice with a Peer

Broadcast interviews can be nerve-racking because the stakes feel so high. What if you say something that gets taken out of context? What if you freeze up and completely fail to perform? And it's all caught on tape!

Being nervous is only natural, but one way to tamp down a serious case of stage fright is to practice. Call on a colleague, a friend, or a family member to take you through your paces. You can give your pseudo-interviewer a list of potential questions and ask him or her to lob them at you. Make sure to give your "interviewer" free license to add his or her own questions to test your ability to handle the unexpected.

I will walk you through a mock interview activity at the end of this chapter.

DURING THE TV INTERVIEW

You've done your homework. You've crafted your messages. You've even practiced saying them during a mock interview. CNN, bring it on. But before the camera starts rolling, here are a few insider tips.

Establishing a Friendly Rapport

If the interview is going to be a taped, sit-down affair, expect the setup to take some time. Once a spot is chosen, the crew will immediately go about creating an impromptu set using whatever is close at hand. Furniture will be moved into position to allow for a comfortable distance between you and the interviewer. You will be asked to take a seat while the crew adjusts the lights that they've now erected on stands around the room.

While you wait, you could just sit there in uncomfortable silence as the reporter looks over his or her notes. Or, you could use that time to establish a friendly rapport prior to the camera being turned on.

Reporters are people, too, with lives beyond their work. Try taking on the interviewer role. Ask neutral questions like, "Where are you from originally?" It usually opens the door to casual conversation, which can serve two purposes: it helps to calm your nerves, and it establishes a more amiable tone.

Checking Yourself in the Mirror

Before the interview starts, check yourself in the mirror. Make sure your shirt is buttoned correctly, your pants are zipped, and your hair is in place, not winging out wildly on one side.

The reporter or videographer may spot that errant poppy seed in your teeth and politely let you know you need to remove it. But there's also a chance they may not because they are busy concentrating on other aspects of the interview.

Take out the guesswork and take on the responsibility to give yourself the once-over.

Realizing When the Camera Is On

You've probably heard the term *off the record*. When it comes to broadcast interviews, there really is no such thing. If there is a camera in the room, consider it to always be on.

Don't wait to be told, "We're rolling." Not all reporters inform their subjects that they are starting the interview. It may sound underhanded, and perhaps sometimes it is. But there are times when it's done for a less nefarious reason. People tend to clam up as soon they are told the official interview is starting.

Sometimes, I would not tell my interview subjects that we were starting to record simply because I saw too often what would happen when I did. The mere mention that the camera was "on" suddenly turned an individual who was normally verbose into someone who was nearly mute. It was almost like saying, "Okay, it's time to get really nervous now." By not signaling the official start, I was able to capture them at their natural best. I used this technique only if the story was a feature, not a hard news story. Not giving a heads-up to the chief of police, for example, would not go over well, but the owner of a Christmas tree farm who was supplying the White House fir didn't mind it a bit.

Different reporters have different standards, and you will not know in advance. Err on the side of caution and consider yourself to be "on" as soon as the reporter walks into the room.

Orally Editing Your Sound Bite

We've already talked about how essential it is to answer concisely, whether it is a live interview or being taped. If it's the latter, there's a way to increase the odds that your carefully crafted sound bite will be used: pause both before and after saying it.

A video editor needs some pad when splicing and dicing the interview into usable segments. While today's tools make the editing process much more precise, if a sound bite has a second of silence on both ends, it is almost too tantalizing to pass up.

As a reporter, I would listen for sound bites during the course of an interview. Once I heard one, I knew I could move on to another topic. Make it easier on both you and your interviewer by speaking in sound bites and highlighting them with pauses.

Controlling the Controllables

You may not be the one holding the microphone or the camera, but you most definitely are the one in control. You dictate the pace and the duration of the interview. After all, without *you*, there is no interview.

Still, you can't control the questions, and there very well may be some you simply don't like. But you *can* control how you answer them. Here are a few suggestions for navigating your way through the most common broadcast interview: a taped sit-down interview.

Pause to Ponder

Don't feel like you have to start answering a question as soon as the reporter utters the last word of it. You do both sides a disservice. You need time to gather your thoughts, so you can give the best possible answer. And if you do articulate an amazing sound bite, don't you want there to be a definite pause before it so the editor can easily pluck it from the recorded interview?

A moment of silence is well worth your time. The reporter will wait, and any dead air will be edited out anyway.

Press Your Own Reset Button

If you find yourself stumbling through an answer, don't feel like you're on a roller coaster and can't get off until it pulls into the gate. Simply stop and explain that you misspoke and you are going to try to answer it again. Give yourself (and the editor) a little pause, and then take another shot at answering the question.

The reporter will be looking for a sound bite that is fully formed, not one that was arrested in the middle of it. That less-than-perfect take will not be used, so feel free to hit the reset rather than settle for an answer that you might not want to hit air.

Keep Your Cool

Most reporters are not your adversaries. They are there to do their job: tell a good story, satisfy their editors, and go home. The easier you make that job, the sooner he or she will be out the door.

However, there are some reporters who try to provoke a reaction from their subjects. You may even feel justified to meet their hostility with your own hostility. *Don't do it.* That reporter may be delighted to include your hissy fit in the story but will somehow *forget* to include his or her own obnoxious behavior that lead up to it. You will look bad and the reporter will remain unscathed.

Answer Every Question as Best You Can

"No comment." Never, ever say those two words to a reporter. It's easily translated to "it's true, and I don't want to talk about it."

You may not want to discuss something. You may even be legally bound to not comment, but if that's the case, you can say something along these lines: "We are not in a position where we can discuss that right now, but when we can, we will be happy to let you know."

I have had the distinct *pleasure* of covering many, many politicians who are masters of the nonanswer. Sure, they say a lot of words that may be tangentially related to the question, but they don't necessarily *answer* the question being asked. As a reporter, it drove me batty because I knew I would not be able to pull any sound bite out of the verbal equivalent of a bob and weave.

Dancing around a question may seem like a good strategy, but it will certainly prolong the interview and annoy the reporter. As an alternative, consider how you might briefly address the question and then transition to another topic that you do want to discuss. This technique is called *bridging* and is a staple of media training.

While many people have been coached on how to bridge, few can do it well. You can easily spot examples of bridging done badly:

someone will offer a perfunctory response to the question and then abruptly change the subject. The key to doing it successfully is transitioning with finesse.

BRAVO FOR BRIDGING

CASE STUDY

In December 2013, Anne Hathaway appeared on the *Today* show to promote her new movie, *Les Misérables*. Unfortunately, the headlines in the days leading up to it were not about the film but about her wardrobe malfunction when she stepped out of her limo at the movie's premiere. A member of the paparazzi snapped a picture that revealed more than she had ever intended, and the photo went viral.

Hathaway knew that Matt Lauer, the *Today* show anchor, would ask her about it, and he did right at the beginning of the interview: "Let's just get it out of the way. You had a little wardrobe malfunction the other night. What is the lesson learned from something like that … other than that you keep smiling, which you always do?"

Hathaway was fully prepared and pulled off the most impressive example of bridging I've ever seen. She talked about how sad she was that the person who took the embarrassing picture didn't delete it and instead opted to sell it. Then, she continued: "I'm sorry that we live in a culture that commodifies sexuality upon unwilling participants. Which brings us back to *Les Mis*, because that's who my character is. She is someone who is forced to sell sex to benefit her child because she has nothing."

I challenge you to find a more artful transition than that.

Hathaway didn't duck the question. She met it head-on, but she managed to address it and quickly move on to what really mattered to her: the film.[2]

AFTER THE TV INTERVIEW

Once the interview is over, make sure the reporter knows how to reach you in case he or she needs clarification or has additional questions. Always keep the reporter's deadline in mind. A return phone call or text after 6 P.M. will do him or her no good if the story aired on the 5 o'clock news.

If you want to cultivate the relationship, send a "thank you" note through text, e-mail, or even snail mail. Media outlets are always looking to build up their stable of experts who can comment on the news of the day. If you'd like to position yourself as a go-to resource, your follow-up note of thanks will help to solidify your potential.

Make sure you watch and record the story. Not only is it important to critique your performance, but it also allows you to assess whether your thoughts were represented accurately and within the proper context. If they weren't, assess the extent of the damage. If the story was factually incorrect, contact that media outlet and demand a retraction or correction.

If you didn't like how you came across but it wasn't a total misrepresentation, consider what you might have done differently that would have led to a more favorable outcome. Did you take too long to get to the point and the most important part never made it into the story? Did you venture into "BS" territory when you just should have told the reporter you didn't have the answer right then but would follow up once you did? Chalk it up to experience, do your own damage control if necessary, and remember to think twice if that same reporter calls again.

INTERVIEWS BY SATELLITE

If you've watched any cable news channel, you know satellite interviews are a necessary ingredient in their programming recipe. Experts are beamed in from all over and appear in their own special squares (à la *Brady Bunch*) or rectangles along with the other virtual panelists.

The rules of engagement for satellite interviews are largely the same as they are for any broadcast interview, with one major difference: you have to visualize your interviewer.

I remember feeling sorry for the people who were brought into our newsroom who were going to be featured on satellite interviews as experts at the request of other media outlets. They were situated in the corner of the newsroom designated for these kinds of engagements, given a few directions, and basically left to their own devices. They always looked a little lost.

Perhaps to relieve my own guilt for not being more helpful to those folks who appeared so out of their element, I am now going to help *you* find your way through a satellite interview.

Introducing the IFB

Most newsrooms have a place designated to accommodate satellite interviews. They are usually pretty bare bones—with a camera, chair, monitor, and microphone. You can expect someone to put the mic on you in the best location available, but you will also be given an earpiece, also known as an IFB.

The acronym *IFB* stands for *interruptible feedback,* and it provides a way for anyone in the control room to talk to someone on air. If you make a living as a broadcast journalist, you probably will have a superfancy IFB that is actually molded to fit your ear, but if not, you will be given a version that is one-size-fits-all.

Your IFB is your lifeline. It is the only way you will know when the show is *live*. It is the only way you will be able to hear the questions from the interviewer. It is the only way you will know when you are clear. You need that IFB to stay in your ear, so don't be dainty with it. "Stick it in your ear" is not an insult in this case—it's a mandate.

The IFB has a wire that will extend either to a wireless transmitter that you will wear on your person or to the set itself. Make sure that wire is tucked behind your head, out of sight. A wire dangling out to the side is distracting for your audience and makes you look unprofessional.

Ask for an IFB check before going live. Someone from the control room will speak in your ear. You want to be sure you can hear what is said clearly and ask for the volume to be turned up or down based on your preferences.

Managing the Monitor

Before you go live, you should check the monitor, which will show you a preview shot of how you are situated within the frame. The camera is usually in a set position, and you can make small adjustments so you are seated squarely. Check your appearance. Look for hair out of place or odd wrinkles in your clothing. Once you are satisfied, ignore the monitor.

Even though you will be conversing with someone during the interview, you have to adopt the same method as you would for a direct-to-camera presentation. Your viewer or your conversation partner is not in the monitor—he or she is through the lens. Therefore, your focus needs to be solely on the camera.

Even though it is almost irresistible to not look at yourself, if you sneak glances at the monitor during the actual interview, you will look unsure and shifty. Force yourself to stay focused on the conversation you are very much a part of and tune out the distractions that might be swirling around you.

When someone was giving an interview via satellite in our newsroom, no one bothered to stop what he or she was doing or even quiet down. Your live interview may not be important to those around you, but it needs to be your *only* priority.

Even if you are not speaking, continue to look into the lens. You never know when your camera is going to be taken live. You don't want to be caught staring off into space.

Waiting for the All-Clear

You may feel like you've said all you have to say, but you are not allowed to get up and leave. You have to stay put until someone tells you through your IFB that the interview is over and you are clear.

Once you have confirmed you are off the air, you can take off your earpiece and unclip the microphone. This last step is often forgotten, and I admit giggling a bit whenever I saw guests get yanked back to the set by the microphone cord as if it were a recoiling dog leash.

Conduct a Mock Interview

ACTIVITY

This exercise will allow you to practice your broadcast interview skills before CNN calls.

WHAT YOU WILL NEED TO COMPLETE THIS EXERCISE

You will need a friend or colleague who is willing to play the role of reporter.

(Continued)

(*Continued*)

You will also need something to record yourself. You can use any of the following:

- Webcam capable of recording to a computer with a playback function
- Smartphone or tablet set to selfie video mode
- Laptop with built-in camera video mode (available on most PCs and Macs)
- Camcorder that has an option for reviewing video clips

You have two options for framing: you can set up the camera so that only you are being recorded, or you can have the camera capture a two-shot with both you and your interviewer in frame.

For most broadcast interviews, the camera will be over the shoulder of the interviewer and pointed just at you.

SCENARIO

Think of something with which you are associated that might garner news coverage. It could be work related, like a product launch or an award. Or it could be related to something you are involved with outside of work, like a charity or a sport. Write down a list of questions a reporter might ask about your chosen subject and give it to your "interviewer."

Instruct your interviewer to add his or her own questions as well and to not just throw softballs. You need practice handling the hostile questions, too.

RECORDING THE INTERVIEW

Hit the record button, and once you're both settled, start the mock interview. Try to keep your answers to that 15-second time frame. Once you feel like you have enough to review, stop recording.

REVIEWING THE INTERVIEW

As you are watching your interview, take note of the following:

- Were you able to keep your answers concise? Use a stopwatch to actually time your answers.
- Did you fidget or gesture so much that it was distracting on camera? If so, think of how you might mitigate the effects. If

your hands were fluttering around the frame, consider keeping them clasped in your lap during an actual interview.

- How successful were you in conveying your key messages? Were you able to say them in a clear and compelling manner?

- Did you ever appear flustered? If so, take note of what threw you off. Knowing what might trip you up will help you to stay on track if that situation arises during a real interview.

CHAPTER TAKEAWAYS

- The first step with a broadcast interview is deciding whether to grant one, based on the reporter and media outlet making the request.

- Find out the focus and angle of the story so you can adequately prepare.

- Develop and simplify talking points, which you can verbalize in a variety of ways.

- Practice speaking in sound bites not longer than 15 seconds.

- If possible, establish a friendly rapport with the reporter in advance.

- Check yourself in the mirror for any appearance gaffes.

- Assume that the camera is always on.

- Orally edit your sound bites by pausing before and after them.

- Keep your cool even if provoked.

- Never say "no comment."

- Bridging is a technique that allows you to address something more negative and then smoothly transition to a related but more positive subject.

- When interviewed via satellite, check the monitor on the set to be sure you are sitting squarely in the frame.

- An IFB is an earpiece you will wear so the control room and your interviewer can speak to you.

- Always look into the lens during a satellite interview until you are told you are clear.
- Unclip your microphone before trying to leave the set. You won't get very far if you don't.

NOTES

1. For an example of how the length of a sound bite has changed over time, see the "The Incredible Shrinking Sound Bite" at http://www.npr.org/2011/01/05/132671410/Congressional-Sound-Bites.
2. You can see the entire interview on YouTube. Here's the URL: https://www.youtube.com/watch?v=TwWSxTiSmfg.

Conclusion: Embrace Communicating through the Camera

No doubt, you did not enter the business world hoping to earn an Oscar or Emmy. The good news is—that's not the expectation.

However, being able to communicate through the camera is becoming an essential skill for everyone. If video hasn't fully invaded your professional space, rest assured it will.

Those who can effectively present on and to the camera raise their personal stock substantially. Becoming one of the faces of your company can lead to greater opportunities within your organization or even widen your career path beyond your current place of employment. With video-conferencing gaining popularity as a first-line hiring tool, your stellar skill on camera may end up landing you your next job.

Speaking on camera can be scary, and many people won't have the confidence to even try it unless they are forced into it. Hopefully, this book has helped to defeat the fear of the unknown and will inspire you to embrace any and every on-camera opportunity that comes your way.

It's lovely to think that simply reading a book will make you a flawless on-camera presenter. It certainly will make you better, but, as with almost anything, practice is key. Performance jitters decrease with familiarity, and your skills will become rusty if you don't use them on a regular basis.

If you are stumped on how to immediately flex your on-camera muscles, here are a few options:

- Suggest holding a videoconference rather than a teleconference for your next meeting. Your fellow participants may initially balk, but you can win them over by highlighting the benefits: you can get more done in a shorter period time if everyone is forced to stay visually accountable.

231

- Instead of *writing* a blog post, record one, using your smartphone. Keep it casual, in tone and production. It'll be refreshing and likely receive more attention than a written version.

- Propose a video series for your company's web site. You could talk about a customer success story or a new product being launched. Instead of having written bios on your team page, consider doing short on-camera versions. It'll be a differentiator and allow potential customers get to know you in a much deeper way.

Get creative. Rethink what's always been put in print and consider whether it might have more impact if it were presented via video. The ways you can leverage your on-camera skills will only grow in number as more and more media channels come on line.

Take the time to study presenters you admire. YouTube and the like provide hours and hours of case studies. Try out some of the techniques you observe, but don't be someone you're not. If it feels contrived, it'll appear fake to your audience. Authenticity is paramount.

Cameras as communication tools are game changers. They provide intimacy and immediacy that no other medium can match. The camera is not your enemy; it's your conduit that allows you to deeply connect with your audience—anywhere, any time. And in this video-driven world, that camera can be a conduit to your professional success.

About the Author

Karin Reed is the CEO of Speaker Dynamics, a communications firm based in Raleigh, North Carolina. She has made a career out of communicating through a camera as an award-winning broadcast journalist, on-camera spokesperson, and executive communications specialist.

Karin has been a trusted trainer and consultant for companies ranging from early-stage start-up to Fortune 500. She empowers her clients, whether they come from the C-suite or the sales force, to speak with ease to any audience on any platform. Her methodology is based on more than 20 years of personal presentation prowess and the understanding that the best speakers are steeped in authenticity.

Index